The
ESSENTIAL
Gardening
Made Easy

Bulbs
for
SPRING
Color

MP

INTERNATIONAL
MASTERS
PUBLISHERS, INC.

Printed and Manufactured in China.

ISBN: 1-892207-15-X

US P 0701 11 002

CONTENTS

WELCOME

The ESSENTIAL
Gardening Made Easy

Bulbs for Spring Color

NOTHING HERALDS THE arrival of spring better than a row of colorful Tulips or a blanket of bright Crocuses. Whether they form the backbone of your flower garden, or provide cheery accents around an entryway, bulbs have a way of commanding attention wherever they're planted. Besides coming in a wide variety of shapes, styles, and colors, bulbs are easy to grow and maintain, which makes them a favorite with both beginning and experienced gardeners.

Generally, the term "bulbs" is used to refer to a variety of plants that store their food materials in a similar way. In addition to true bulbs, other plants that are grouped in the bulb category include corms, tubers, tuber-corms, tuberous roots, and rhizomes. Bulbs are grouped once more according to the season in which they bloom—spring bulbs, which are usually planted in the fall, or summer and fall bulbs, which are usually planted in the spring.

Spring bulbs—the subject of this book—are the most popular kind of bulbs. Most notably they include Irises, Crocuses, Hyacinths, and many varieties of Narcissi and Tulips. You'll learn all about these and many other bulbs in this volume of *The Essential Gardening Made Easy*. So, whether your goal is a windowbox of Triumph Tulips or a garden border of fragrant Dutch Hyacinths, you'll receive all the information you need to create a beautiful, successful spring garden. From practical planting and aftercare advice to creative planting schemes, you'll be delighted when you discover that creating the bulb garden of your dreams is easier than you think!

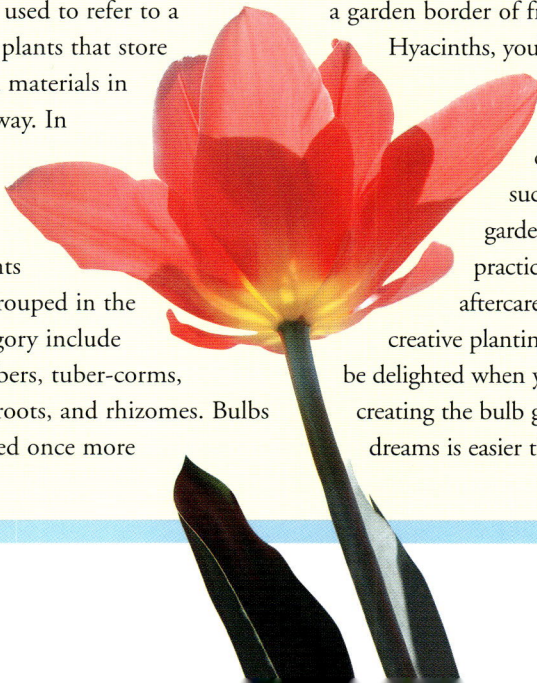

creating a bulb garden
that complements
your landscape

BULBS ARE VERY VERSATILE AND FLOURISH IN A VARIETY OF SETTINGS. Many bulbs work well in more formal beds, where their size, color, and shape are used to carry out a specific design concept. Tulips have a classic appeal and look best when grouped together to form solid blocks of color. They come in an enormous range of colors and varieties and are successful in designs where repetition and balance are the key considerations. Bulbs can play important roles in a range of stylized landscape designs, putting on spectacular spring shows when planted with other bulbs and early perennials.

One planting technique, called a "naturalized effect" is to plant bulbs randomly in a wildflower garden or over an area of your lawn to imitate how they might appear in the wild. This works particularly well with Crocuses used as groundcover or Poppy Anemones scattered in an informal woodland-type garden. Daffodils also lend themselves well to naturalized settings because they flourish in both full sun and partial shade and will thrive under deciduous trees or in woodland borders.

Bulbs that have dramatic shapes, such as Irises and Lilies, and bulbs that are especially fragrant, like Hyacinths, are often grown for the specific purpose of cutting and displaying indoors. They make striking fresh-flower arrangements, and allow you to enjoy the wonderful colors and scents of your garden in any room of your home. If you're growing bulbs for a cut-flower garden, plant the bulbs in rows. This will make it easier to weed, maintain, and eventually cut the flowers.

If you have a penchant for bright, primary colors, bulbs will quickly win your heart. Bulbs in primary colors have a simple, arresting appeal and look great in areas where they can be seen from inside the home as well as outside. Consider planting bulbs near the house where they can be viewed from a picture window, or plant them in

a burst of spring

Bulbs have been around for many centuries. Most of them originated in the Mediterranean, where the winters were too cold and the summers were too hot for the plants to survive. Thus, they adapted by learning to bloom in the spring and fall. They also carry all the food and energy they need to survive with them, conveniently stored in a ball of dense leaves that makes up their bulblike structure. True bulbs are perennials and will produce beautiful blooms year after year.

windowboxes or containers placed on the front steps, the deck or the patio. Before you do any planting, make sure you map out your landscaping plans on paper. The most important consideration is that your new plans complement your existing landscape.

Take some time to walk around your yard before you do your actual planting. Do you have areas that receive full sun, or lots of trees that create a shadier environment? Is your house on a hill where run-off might be a problem—or, are there several depressions in your yard where water might collect and make the soil too soggy? The more you evaluate your current landscape and plan around the natural conditions of your yard, the more successful your garden will be.

The next step is to start with good-quality bulbs. A high percentage of spring bulbs are imported from the Netherlands and have been grown under strict conditions so they arrive in good shape. Still, you should check to make sure they do not have any soft spots or signs of mold. Bulbs should be smooth, firm, and heavy for their size. Keep in mind that larger bulbs—which produce larger flowers—are more expensive, as are new cultivars.

It's best to plant bulbs soon after you purchase them. Plant spring bulbs in September or October because this gives them time to develop roots before the ground gets too cold. Once they're planted, your work is pretty much done—come springtime you can sit back, relax, and enjoy the show.

a pretty tulip bed

GARDEN IDEAS & INSPIRATION

Ideas for a
Dutch Spring Garden

For a parade of riotous color, fill a bed with spring bulbs and continue the show through summer with annual and perennial groundcovers.

Brilliant Bulbs for Spring

Create a no-fail spring show by planting masses of spring-blooming Dutch bulbs in fall.

Hardy, spring-blooming bulbs make it easy to celebrate spring. For the greatest impact, plant blocks of each bulb to create masses of vivid color. To ensure that an entire block of flowers blooms in unison, plant them all at the same depth, since different planting depths will result in staggered bloom times.

Hardy bulbs thrive in full sun or in the spring sunshine under deciduous trees. Since they disappear after flowering—foliage and all—combine them with shallow-rooted, sun- or shade-loving annuals, perennials, or groundcovers, depending on the type of site you have.

SINGLE EARLY TULIP 'KEIZERSKROON'
H: 10-14 in., S: 6-8 in.; blooms striped with yellow and orange-red; broad, blade-like leaves; zones 3-8

TRIUMPH TULIP 'JOHN GIANT'
H: 16-20 in., S: 8-10 in.; very dark red, almost black, flowers; blade-like, fleshy, blue-green leaves; zones 3-8

SINGLE EARLY TULIP 'BEAUTY OF VOLENDAM'
H: 12-14 in., S: 6-8 in.; white flowers striped with crimson red; broad, blade-like, blue-green leaves; zones 3-8

GRAPE HYACINTHS
H and S: 4-6 in.; fragrant, Grape-like clusters of small, blue flowers; grass-like leaves from fall to spring; zones 2-9

TRIUMPH TULIP 'GARDEN PARTY'
H: 16-18 in., S: 8-10 in.; white petals with wide, red edges; blade-like, fleshy, blue-green leaves; zones 3-8

FOSTERIANA TULIP 'WHITE EMPEROR'
H: 12-14 in., S: 8-10 in.; pure white flowers; broad, blade-like leaves; zones 3-8

DARWIN TULIP 'APELDOORN'
H: 18-24 in., S: 8-10 in.; flame red flowers on tall stems; broad, blade-like, blue-green leaves; zones 3-8

REMBRANDT TULIPS
H: 24-30 in., S: 8-10 in.; petals striped with contrasting colors, including white, red, and yellow; broad, blade-like leaves; zones 3-8

1 **Use stakes and string** to mark a 3 ft. wide bed in lawn next to a path. Spread a tarp on the lawn and dig out soil to a depth of 9 in.

2 **Loosen the soil** in the bottom of the bed and work in 1 in. of compost. Arrange Tulip bulbs in blocks, spacing bulbs 6-8 in. apart.

3 **Carefully fill in** over Tulips with 4 in. of soil. Arrange clumps of Grape Hyacinth bulbs, spaced 4 in. apart, between Tulips.

4 **Carefully replace** rest of soil to cover Grape Hyacinth bulbs. Topdress the soil with dried manure to fertilize. Add a layer of mulch.

5 **In early spring,** as leaves begin emerging, topdress with bulb fertilizer. Leave foliage untouched until it turns yellow.

6 **As leaves yellow,** cut them back. Plant annuals and perennials between the clumps to fill the planting with flowers for summer.

More Plants for a Dutch Spring Garden

TYPE	PLANT	DESCRIPTION
SMALL BULBS	Snowdrops *(far left)*	White early spring flowers; grass-like leaves; 6 in.; zones 3-9
	Oxalis adenophylla (left)	Pink-and-white late spring flowers; gray-green leaves; 4 in.; zones 5-9
	Iris reticulata 'Harmony'	Dark blue flowers in early spring; grass-like leaves; 6 in.; zones 4-9
	Snow Crocus 'Prins Claus'	Purple-and-white early spring blooms; thin leaves; 6 in.; zones 4-9
LARGE BULBS	Daffodil 'Pink Pride' *(far left)*	White-and-pink mid-spring flowers; strap-like leaves; 8 in.; zones 4-9
	Hyacinth 'Pink Perfection' *(left)*	Fragrant, pink early spring flowers; strap-like leaves; 8 in.; zones 6-9
	Dutch Iris 'Romano'	Purple-and-gold late spring flowers; strap-like leaves; 18 in.; zones 6-9
	Crown Imperial 'Lutea'	Yellow early spring flower clusters; narrow leaves; 3 ft.; zones 6-9
GROUNDCOVERS FOR SUN	Verbena 'Blaze' *(far left)*	Small, scarlet spring to fall flowers; dark green leaves; 9 in.; all zones
	Harebell 'Alba' *(left)*	White summer to fall bells; round leaves; 10 in.; zones 4-9
	Lobelia 'Blue Splash'	Lilac-blue summer blooms; bronze leaves; 9 in.; annual; all zones
	Zinnia 'Lollipop Series'	Yellow, red, or white summer flowers; 10 in.; annual; all zones
GROUNDCOVERS FOR SHADE	Coleus 'Brilliant Mix' *(far left)*	Pink, maroon, green, yellow, and white foliage; 1 ft.; annual; all zones
	Impatiens 'Super Elfin Mix' *(left)*	Pink, white, or red summer flowers; oval leaves; 10 in.; annual; all zones
	Red Epimedium	Small, red spring flowers; attractive, heart-shaped leaves; 1 ft.; zones 4-8
	Hosta 'Aphrodite'	Fragrant, white trumpets in summer; large, green leaves; 2 ft.; zones 3-9

Ideas for
Bold Blocks of Bulb Color

To paint the landscape with brush strokes of long-lasting spring color, plant bulbs in fall that bloom in early, middle, and late spring.

Dazzling Spring Hues

For a garden that is dramatic in spring and attractive right to frost, combine bulbs with perennials and annuals.

Taking time to plant hardy bulbs in fall will yield an enormous dividend of vibrant color come spring. By selecting the right bulbs to plant, you can extend the display for nearly two months. Instead of planting one variety of Tulip or Daffodil, plant a mix of varieties described as blooming in early, mid-, and late spring. That way, your display will begin as the snow melts and continue until the first summer-blooming perennials begin to flower. Bulbs need spring sun (partial shade in summer is fine) and soil that is well drained.

To fill the bed with color through summer, overplant bulbs with annuals and perennials that will fill in as the bulb foliage fades.

DARWIN TULIP 'GENERAL EISENHOWER'
H: 20-24 in., S: 6-8 in.; glowing red flowers in mid-spring; blade-like, blue-green leaves; zones 3-8

HYACINTH 'CARNEGIE'
H: 8 in., S: 5 in.; dense clusters of intensely fragrant, white flowers in early to mid-spring; strap-like leaves; zones 6-9

FRINGED TULIP 'NORANDA'
H: 16-24 in., S: 6-8 in.; dark red blooms with orange fringe in mid- to late spring; blade-like, green leaves; zones 3-8

TRIUMPH TULIP 'AMBASSADOR'
H: 16-18 in., S: 6-8 in.; bright red midspring blooms; blade-like, blue-green leaves; zones 3-8

**DARWIN TULIP
'PRESIDENT KENNEDY'**
H: 20-24 in., S: 6-8 in.;
bright yellow blooms
in mid-spring; blade-like,
blue-green leaves;
zones 3-8

**HEATH
'PINK SPANGLES'**
H: 6 in., S: 18 in.;
mounds of tiny, pink,
bell-shaped flowers in
spring; needle-like,
evergreen leaves;
zones 5-8

**SIBERIAN
SQUILL**
H and S: 4-6 in.;
clusters of
brilliant blue,
bell-shaped
flowers in
early spring;
strap-like
leaves;
zones 3-9

**DAFFODIL
'YELLOW
CHEERFULNESS'**
H: 16 in., S: 5 in.;
clusters of fragrant, double,
yellow flowers in mid- to
late spring; strap-like
leaves; zones 3-9

PLANTING & AFTERCARE

1 **In late summer** or fall, mark a 3 ft. by 8 ft. bed using stakes and string. Remove grass and dig out the soil to 10 in. deep.

2 **Loosen soil** in bottom of bed with garden fork and work in 1 in. of compost. Space Tulip bulbs 4-6 in. apart in drifts of solid colors.

3 **Replace 2 in.** of soil; cover bulbs carefully so pointed ends stay facing up. Plant Daffodils and Hyacinths 4-5 in. apart on top of Tulips.

4 **Carefully replace** the remaining soil. Along one edge, set Siberian Squill bulbs 3 in. deep, 4 in. apart. Plant Heath 1 ft. behind Squills.

5 **Water** thoroughly to settle the soil. Mulch bed with 2-4 in. of chopped leaves. Fertilize in spring just before flowers appear.

6 **Cut back bulb** foliage after it turns completely yellow in spring. Interplant annuals and perennials to add color through the summer.

Ideas for Bold Blocks of Bulb Color

More Plants for Bold Bulb Color

TYPE	PLANT	DESCRIPTION
EARLY SPRING	Tulip 'Red Riding Hood' *(far left)*	Bright red-orange blooms; maroon-striped foliage; 10 in.; zones 3-8
	Winter Aconite *(left)*	Golden flowers; ruffled, leafy collar under flowers; 6 in.; zones 4-9
	Grape Hyacinth 'Blue Spike'	Clusters of double, blue flowers; grass-like leaves; 6 in.; zones 3-9
	Snow Crocus 'Blue Bird'	Flowers white inside, lilac outside; grass-like leaves; 6 in.; zones 4-9
MIDSPRING	Striped Squill *(far left)*	Clusters of pale blue flowers; strap-like leaves; 6 in.; zones 3-9
	White Dog-tooth Violet *(left)*	Nodding, white flowers; slender, flat leaves; 10-12 in.; zones 4-8
	Tulipa saxatilis	Small, pink-and-yellow blooms; strap-like leaves; 8 in.; zones 3-8
	Jonquilla Daffodil 'Pipit'	Nodding, pale yellow flowers; strap-like leaves; 8 in.; zones 4-9
LATE SPRING	Foxtail Lily *(far left)*	Bold spikes of tiny, yellow flowers; strap-like leaves; 3 ft.; zones 5-9
	Allium unifolium (left)	Clusters of small, pink flowers; grass-like leaves; 8 in.; zones 4-8
	Camassia 'Blue Danube'	Spikes of dark blue flowers; strap-like leaves; 4 ft.; zones 3-10
	Parrot Tulip 'Texas Gold'	Ruffled, golden yellow flowers; blue-green leaves; 20 in.; zones 3-8
BULB COMPANIONS	Vinca 'Bowles Variety' *(far left)*	Dark green, evergreen leaves; deep blue spring flowers; 6 in.; zones 4-9
	Epimedium 'Rose Queen' *(left)*	Heart-shaped leaves; small, pink flowers in spring; 15 in.; zones 4-8
	Hosta 'Wide Brim'	Green leaves edged in white; lilac summer flowers; 18 in.; zones 3-9
	Lungwort 'Mrs. Moon'	Silver-spotted leaves; tubular, pink and blue flowers; 18 in.; zones 3-8

Ideas for
Planting Around a Tree

For an easy-care planting under a tree, carpet the ground with shade-loving bulbs and flowers that provide colorful blooms and lush foliage.

A Flowering Tapestry

To create a shade garden that is alive with color and texture from spring to fall, combine plants that bloom at different seasons.

A lush carpet of hardy spring bulbs starts the year off with bright colors for this planting in the shade of a tree. Interplanting bulbs and perennials that bloom at different seasons will extend the show right through fall. As the bulbs finish flowering, emerging foliage and flowers of later-blooming plants will take center stage.

Bulbs and perennials with colorful foliage—or leaves that are simply attractive over a long season—are especially important in any shade garden. They provide lush, green color and rich texture that set off the flowers to their best advantage.

SPRING STARFLOWER (IPHEION UNIFLORUM) H: 4-6 in., S: 2-3 in.; star-shaped, violet-blue or white flowers in spring; pale green leaves smell of Onions when crushed; zones 6-9

PERIWINKLE (VINCA MINOR) H: 5-6 in., S: 1-3 ft.; lilac-blue flowers in spring; spreading stems with small, oval, dark green leaves; excellent evergreen groundcover for shade; zones 4-9

DAFFODIL 'MOUNT HOOD' H: 16-18 in., S: 9-12 in.; early spring-blooming bulb with trumpet-shaped blooms that open creamy yellow and turn white; strap-like leaves; zones 3-9

DAFFODIL 'RIP VAN WINKLE'
H and S: 6-8 in.; early spring-blooming bulb with frilly, double, yellow blooms; strap-like leaves; zones 4-9

1 Clear weeds and grass from a 6 ft. radius under tree, working carefully to avoid disturbing tree roots. Spread 2 in. of compost.

2 In fall, arrange Daffodil and Spring Starflower bulbs in natural-looking clumps. Space bulbs 6-8 in. apart and plant 8 in. deep.

3 In fall, or in spring north of zone 7, soak Poppy Anemone tubers overnight in water. Plant 3-4 in. apart and as deep.

4 In spring or fall, plant Periwinkle between clumps of bulbs. Space plants 1-2 ft. apart and spread runners in all directions.

POPPY ANEMONE
H: 1 ft., S: 10-12 in.; showy, cup-shaped spring flowers in brilliant red, pink, or purple; deeply cut, Fern-like leaves; grown from a knobby tuber; grown as annual north of zone 7; zones 7-10

5 After bulbs bloom in each season, do not remove remaining foliage until it has turned yellow. Remove weeds as they appear.

6 Fill between bulbs with annuals and perennials. Mulch bed with chopped leaves to control weeds and keep soil moist.

21

More Plants for Planting Around a Tree

SEASON		PLANT	DESCRIPTION
WINTER		Winter Aconite *(far left)*	Cup-shaped, yellow flowers; glossy, green leaves; 2-4 in.; zones 4-9
		Lenten Rose *(left)*	Late-winter flowers open green, then turn white or purple; 2 ft.; zones 4-9
		Winterberry	Deciduous shrub with bright red winter berries; 6 ft.; zones 4-9
		Christmas Fern	Evergreen Fern; glossy, deep green fronds; 2 ft.; zones 3-9
SPRING		Bergenia 'Siberia' *(far left)*	Rose-purple spring flowers; large, evergreen leaves; 1 ft.; zones 3-8
		Ajuga pyramidalis (left)	Semi-evergreen groundcover with blue flower spikes; 6 in.; zones 3-8
		Woodland Forget-me-not	Blue flowers with yellow centers; lance-like leaves; 8 in.; zones 3-8
		Crocus sieberi 'Tricolor'	Purple, white, and orange blooms; grass-like leaves; 6 in.; zones 4-9
SUMMER		Wild Columbine *(far left)*	Red-and-yellow flowers; blue-green leaves; 1-3 ft.; zones 3-9
		Jack-in-the-pulpit *(left)*	Green or purple, hooded flower; lobed leaves; 1-2 ft.; zones 4-9
		Caladium 'White Christmas'	White foliage with bright green veins; 20 in.; tender bulb; all zones
		Allegheny Foam Flower	Spikes of white spring flowers; Maple-like leaves; 1 ft.; zones 3-9
FALL		New England Aster *(far left)*	Starry, pink-purple flowers from late summer to fall; 3 ft.; zones 4-8
		Blue Fescue *(left)*	Ornamental, blue-gray grass; showy fall seedheads; 4-18 in.; zones 4-9
		Impatiens 'Elfin'	Pink, white, or red flowers; dark leaves; 15 in.; annual; all zones
		Gentiana septemfida	Bright blue flowers; bright green leaves; 8 in.; zones 3-8

Ideas for
Tiers of Spring Color

*For an early-season display, plant masses
of flowers together in a bold, horizontal
pattern of colorful blooms.*

Vivid Ribbons of Color

Grouping flowers of similar heights and hues lets you paint brushstrokes of color through a garden.

This garden owes its bold appeal to mass plantings of flowers that fill it with striking color. In group plantings, flowers are generally spaced closer than they normally would be, to ensure that the blooms create an unbroken sheet of color. This planting uses vibrant flowers in formal rows for a horizontal color scheme. Within the rows, consider alternating masses of bloom color for a unique spin on the tier-like effect. All the flowers in this garden thrive in full sun to light shade and rich, well-drained soil.

It is easy to scale down large plantings like this one to fit any site in your yard. Just plant smaller or narrower blocks of each flower color.

TULIP
'LEEN VAN DER MARK'
H: 18 in., S: 8 in.; bright red, white-edged petals, with darker red interiors; blooms in mid-spring; large, fleshy, blue-green leaves; zones 3-8

PANSY
'ICEQUEEN SERIES'
H and S: 6-8 in.; rounded, flat, bright petals in shades of yellow, red, purple, pink, or orange marked with face-like blotches in velvety brown or black; blooms from early spring to summer; oval leaves; annual; all zones

PANSY 'LYRIC WHITE'
H and S: 6-8 in.; rounded, flat, white blooms from early spring to summer; small, yellow centers and face-like blotches in maroon or brown; oval leaves; annual; all zones

1 **In late summer** or fall, remove grass and weeds from a 10 ft. by 8 ft. area. Turn over soil, spread 2 in. of compost, and dig it in.

2 **In fall,** plant Tulips 6 in. apart in staggered rows. Be sure to plant all bulbs 8 in. deep or they will bloom at uneven heights.

3 **In early spring,** plant a row of Pansies in front of Tulips with alternating 3-4 ft. patches of 'Icequeen', 'Joker', and 'Lyric White'.

4 **Plant another row** of alternating Pansies in front of the first, but plant in a different sequence to create a changing color pattern.

PANSY 'JOKER'
H and S: 6-8 in.; rounded, flat, blue to purple petals with small, yellow centers or face-like blotches in purple-black or white; blooms from early spring to summer; oval leaves; annual; all zones

5 **Allow Tulip foliage** to turn completely yellow before trimming. The dying foliage serves as food for next year's blooms.

6 **Remove spent Pansy** flowers. In summer, cut plants back by half when blooming stops to encourage growth and fall flowers.

Ideas for **Tiers of Spring Color**

More Plants for Tiers of Spring Color

COLOR	PLANT	DESCRIPTION
BLUE & PURPLE	Tulip 'Attila' *(far left)*	Violet-purple flowers; broad, sword-shaped leaves; 16 in.; zones 3-8
	Crocus 'Flower Record' *(left)*	Cup-shaped, deep purple blooms; grass-like leaves; 4-6 in.; zones 3-9
	Hyacinth 'Delft Blue'	Pale blue flower clusters; strap-like leaves; 8 in.; zones 6-9
	Iris reticulata 'Harmony'	Purple-and-orange flowers; narrow, blue-green leaves; 6 in.; zones 4-9
RED & PINK	Peony 'Jules Elie' *(far left)*	Satiny, crimson, 7 in. flowers; deeply cut leaves; 3 ½ ft.; zones 4-8
	Bleeding-heart *(left)*	Pink, heart-shaped flowers; blue-green leaves; 2 ½ ft.; zones 2-9
	Anemone 'De Caen'	Cup-shaped, red or pink flowers; Fern-like leaves; 1 ft.; zones 7-10
	Cyclamen coum	Tiny, crimson flowers; silver, heart-shaped leaves; 4 in.; zones 5-9
YELLOW & ORANGE	Daffodil 'Mount Hood' *(far left)*	Pale yellow flower turns white; strap-like leaves; 18 in.; zones 4-9
	Primrose 'Magnus Hybrid Mix' *(left)*	Mix of shades including red-orange and gold blooms; 6 in.; zones 5-7
	Crown Imperial 'Aurora'	Clusters of red-orange flowers; narrow, green leaves; 3 ft.; zones 6-9
	Witch Hazel 'Arnold's Promise'	Ribbon-like, yellow flower clusters; orange leaves in fall; 20 ft.; zones 5-8
WHITE	Moss Phlox 'May Snow' *(far left)*	Mat-like, white-flowered groundcover; needle-like leaves; 6 in.; zones 2-9
	White Grape Hyacinths *(left)*	Bell-shaped, white flower clusters; strap-like leaves; 6 in.; zones 3-9
	Fothergilla gardenii	White, bottlebrush-like flowers; oval, blue-green leaves; 4 ft.; zones 5-8
	Double Snowdrops	Delicate, white flowers; thin, strap-like leaves; 6 in.; zones 3-9

Ideas for a
Shady Spring Bulb Design

For a shade garden that is virtually guaranteed to be filled with showstopping color come spring, plant masses of hardy bulbs in fall.

A Blanket of Bright Blooms

Hardy spring bulbs thrive in sites under deciduous trees, which are shady in summer but sunny in spring.

Tulips, Frittilaries, Daffodils, and other hardy bulbs can fill a woodland site with sun-splashed color for weeks in the spring. Although these plants need sun to bloom their best, sites under deciduous trees are ideal for them because hardy spring bulbs need full sun only in the springtime. By the time most trees produce their leaves, the bulbs are already going dormant.

Let your trees—and their roots—help plan your shady spring bulb design. Plant around roots to avoid damaging them. For an attractive display all season long, mix in shade-loving Ferns and Hostas, which will carpet the ground below trees with foliage all summer.

GRECIAN WINDFLOWER 'WHITE SPLENDOR'
H: 3-4 in., S: 4-6 in.; showy, Daisy-like, white flowers with yellow centers in early spring; deeply cut, Fern-like leaves; zones 4-8

GREIGII TULIP 'PINOCCHIO'
H and S: 10 in.; scarlet flowers with gold centers and white-edged petals in early spring; attractive, maroon-striped leaves; zones 3-7

**CROWN IMPERIAL
'LUTEA MAXIMA'**
H: 2-4 ft., S: 9-12 in.;
clusters of showy, bell-
like, gold flowers in
early spring; a tuft of
leaves grows above
flowers; zones 5-9

CROWN IMPERIAL 'AURORA'
H: 2-4 ft., S: 1 ft.; bell-like,
red-orange, early spring
flower clusters; a tuft of
leaves grows above
flowers; zones 5-9

**TULIP
'RED EMPEROR'**
H: 2 ½ ft., S: 1 ft.;
brilliant red flowers
with yellow bases in
early to mid-spring;
strap-like, gray-green
leaves; zones 3-8

PLANTING & AFTERCARE

1 In fall, dig a bed 8-10 in. deep in a free-form pattern around trees. Work carefully, and try to avoid damaging tree roots.

2 Work 1 in. of compost into bed. Space Tulip bulbs 6 in. apart around base of tree and at the middle edge of bed. Refill bed.

3 Soak Windflower tubers overnight. Plant between Tulip patches, 3 in. deep, 4-5 in. apart. Place the tubers on their sides.

4 For best results, plant Crown Imperials early in fall. Group three to five bulbs together at back of bed; plant 6 in. deep, and 8-10 in. apart.

5 Water thoroughly after planting. Spread ¼ in. of well-rotted manure over beds. Do not put manure in holes with bulbs.

6 Mulch the planting area with 2-3 in. of chopped leaves or Pine needles to keep the soil moist and discourage weeds.

More Spring Bulbs for Shade

BULB	VARIETY	DESCRIPTION
DAFFODILS	Daffodil 'Tahiti' *(far left)*	Double, yellow-and-orange flowers; strap-like leaves; 18 in.; zones 4-9
	Daffodil 'Geranium' *(left)*	Fragrant, white-and-orange flowers; strap-like leaves; 14 in.; zones 4-9
	Daffodil 'February Gold'	Extra-early, yellow flowers; strap-like leaves; 14 in.; zones 4-9
	Daffodil 'Las Vegas'	Yellow cups with white petals; strap-like leaves; 18 in.; zones 4-9
TULIPS	Tulip 'Apeldoorn' *(far left)*	Large, red Darwin Tulip; broad, blue-green leaves; 24 in.; zones 3-8
	T. turkestanica *(left)*	Delicate clusters of white flowers; blue-green leaves; 8 in.; zones 3-8
	Tulip 'Big Smile'	Large, yellow Darwin Tulip; broad, blue-green leaves; 30 in.; zones 3-8
	Tulip 'Red Riding Hood'	Scarlet Gregii Tulip; maroon-striped foliage; 10 in.; zones 3-8
CROCUSES	Crocus 'Snow Storm' *(far left)*	Pure white flowers; gold stamens; grassy leaves; 3-4 in.; zones 4-9
	Crocus vernus 'Pickwick' *(left)*	Purple-streaked, white flowers; grassy leaves; 3-4 in.; zones 4-8
	Crocus sieberi 'Firefly'	Deep purple flowers with orange stamens; 2-3 in.; zones 5-8
	Crocus angustifolius	Deep gold flowers; long, grassy leaves; 2 in.; zones 3-9
IRISES	Japanese Iris 'Marhigo' *(far left)*	Large, white flowers with purple edges; 2 ft.; zones 5-9
	Dutch Iris 'Blue Sensation' *(left)*	Purple-blue blooms with gold accents; tall leaves; 18 in.; zones 3-9
	Siberian Iris 'Little White'	Pure white flowers; grass-like leaves; 15 in.; zones 5-9
	Iris reticulata 'Harmony'	Sky blue flowers with yellow markings; 4-6 in.; zones 5-9

Ideas for a
Bearded Iris Bed

*Create a dramatic early summer show
by filling a bed with sword-leaved Bearded Irises
in a rainbow of striking, eye-catching colors.*

Brilliant, Rich Colors

Bearded Irises bear stunning flowers in so many different hues and combinations you can plant exactly the colors you prefer.

To select Bearded Irises for an effective design, it helps to know a bit about the ruffled, fragrant flowers. Bearded Irises have two types of petals that can be the same or different colors. The upright petals are called standards; the ones that trail downward are called falls. The falls have a fuzzy beard in the center that is sometimes a contrasting color.

For the best effect, select six to ten different varieties in different colors. Also try to combine Irises that bloom at different times for continuous flowers from late spring through early summer. Reblooming Irises, which bloom in early summer and again in fall, are now available. All require full sun and well-drained soil.

IRIS 'ROYAL OAK'
H: 3 ½-4 ft., S: 3-4 ft.; reddish brown standards and bluish mauve falls; orange-brown beards; blooms in midseason; sword-shaped leaves; zones 3-9

IRIS 'ENNERDALE'
H and S: 3-4 ft.; pale yellow standards and falls with creamy centers and pale yellow margins; white beards; blooms in midseason; sword-shaped leaves; zones 3-9

IRIS 'ESTER FAY'
H and S: 3-4 ft.; pale, apricot-pink standards and falls with contrasting orange beards; blooms in midseason; sword-shaped leaves; zones 3-9

IRIS 'JANE PHILLIPS'
H and S: 3-4 ft.; delicate, lilac-blue standards and falls; white beards; blooms in mid-season; sword-shaped leaves; zones 3-9

IRIS 'MOON JOURNEY'
H: 3 ½-4 ft., S: 3-4 ft.; white standards with pale, lemon yellow falls; light yellow-orange beards; blooms in midseason; sword-shaped leaves; zones 3-9

IRIS 'STATEN ISLAND'
H: 3 ½-4 ft., S: 3-4 ft.; golden yellow standards and orange-brown falls edged with yellow; orange-yellow beards; blooms in midseason; sword-shaped leaves; zones 3-9

1 **In late summer or fall,** clear a 4 ft. wide by 10 ft. long bed in a site with full sun. Spread 2 in. of compost and dig in to a depth of 1 ft.

2 **Plant** all Bearded Irises in late summer or early fall. Set the fleshy rhizomes so half to one quarter sits above the soil level.

3 **Arrange Irises** in clumps of two to three of the same variety for the best show. Space the rhizome pieces 1 ½-2 ft. apart.

4 **Water the bed** thoroughly but do not mulch. In spring, use stakes and string to hold the heavy bloom stalks upright.

5 **Inspect foliage** for tunnels in leaves. Pinch the tunnels to kill iris borers. Cut back leaves in fall and discard to reduce borers.

6 **Divide plants** every few years in late summer. If hollowed out rhizomes are evident, discard; replant healthy Irises in new location.

More Plants for a Bearded Iris Bed

TYPE		PLANT	DESCRIPTION
EARLY		'Victoria Falls' *(far left)*	Lavender-blue standards and falls; white beards; 36 in.; zones 3-9
		'Amos Sherard' *(left)*	Deep purple standards and falls; violet beards; 36 in.; zones 3-9
		'Jessie Viette'	White standards and yellow falls; yellow beards; 36 in.; zones 3-9
		'Lady Friend'	Rose red standards and falls; orange beards; 36 in.; zones 3-9
MIDSEASON		'Bride's Halo' *(far left)*	White, yellow-edged standards and falls; gold beards; 36 in.; zones 3-9
		'Beverly Sills' *(left)*	Ruffled, pink standards and falls; pink beards; 36 in.; zones 3-9
		'Edith Wolford'	Yellow standards and purple falls; orange beards; 35 in.; zones 3-9
		'Silverado'	Ruffled, pale lilac standards and falls; white beards; 38 in.; zones 3-9
LATE		'Pride of Ireland' *(far left)*	Yellow-green standards and falls; yellow beards; 38 in.; zones 3-9
		'Fall Fiesta' *(left)*	White standards, amber-orange falls; yellow beards; 36 in.; zones 3-9
		'Big Dipper'	Ruffled, golden standards and falls; orange beards; 36 in.; zones 3-9
		'Paradise'	Ruffled, pink standards and falls; orange beards; 36 in.; zones 3-9
REBLOOMING		'Golden Encore' *(far left)*	Golden yellow standards and falls; gold beards; 35 in.; zones 3-9
		'Chaste White' *(left)*	Pure white standards and falls; white beards; 28 in.; zones 3-9
		'Autumn Bugler'	Violet standards; dark purple falls; purple beards; 28 in.; zones 3-9
		'Lady Emma'	Yellow standards and falls; yellow beards; 24 in.; zones 3-9

Ideas for a Multicolored
Late Spring Bed

With a little planning, you can create a flower bed to keep your garden vibrant long after the first burst of spring color has faded.

Extending a Spring Rainbow

Use late-season bloomers for an explosion of color that will carry the garden into summer.

The first flush of early spring blooms can be the most exciting in your garden, but these flowers are often short-lived. This garden design provides long-lasting, late-season spring color for a smooth transition into summer.

Provide wonderful color from spring bulbs with late-blooming varieties of Tulips and Daffodils—flowers that are traditionally associated with early spring. This bed features an evergreen backbone, supplied by a planting of low-growing Japanese Holly.

TULIP 'DREAMING MAID'
H: 16-18 in., S: 6 in.; rose-lavender, long-lasting blooms edged with white in mid-spring; zones 3-8

MUSTARD (BRASSICA NIGRA)
H and S: 3 ft.; tiny, gold flowers until mid-summer; annual; all zones

SEDUM 'BRILLIANT'
H: 2 ft., S: 12-18 in.; large, fleshy, gray leaves; deep pink flowers from late summer to fall; zones 4-9

DAFFODIL 'ST. KEVERNE'
H: 18 in., S: 6 in.; white blooms in early to mid-spring; spiky green foliage lasts into summer; zones 3-9

DWARF JAPANESE HOLLY
H: 2 ft., S: 4 ft.; compact shrub; glossy, emerald leaves; red fall berries; zones 6-8

PANSY
H: 6-8 in., S: 8 in.; red, white, purple, pink, or gold five-petaled blooms; annual; all zones

TULIP 'EASTER FIRE'
H: 14-16 in., S: 6 in.;
bright red blooms in late
spring; kelly green leaves;
zones 3-8

1 **Lay out bed's** shape with a garden hose or rope. Use a spade to cut out the shape from turf, making bed at least 3 ft. wide.

2 **Dig up** entire area about 1 ft. deep, adding a 4 in. layer of compost. Plant two to three irregular groupings of three Hollies in middle.

3 **In fall,** plant Tulips and Daffodils in holes. Plant 8-10 in. deep in masses of a dozen or more along rear of bed. Space bulbs 4 in. apart.

4 **In early spring,** set out Mustard and Sedum to fill spaces in middle of bed. Use groupings of four or five for the greatest impact.

5 **Edge front** of bed with a row of Pansies. When selecting, buy a diverse range of Pansy colors, but make sure at least half are yellow.

6 **Feed bulbs** with a 5-10-5, all-purpose granular fertilizer. Water and apply an organic mulch, such as shredded pine bark.

Ideas for a Multicolored Late Spring Bed

More Plants for Late Spring Color

TYPE		PLANT	DESCRIPTION
SHRUBS		Dwarf Flowering Almond *(far left)*	Small, glossy leaves; profusion of pink flowers; 30 in.; zones 2-8
		Daphne retusa (left)	Glossy, green leaves covered with pink-white flowers; 3 ft.; zones 7-9
		Spanish Gorse	Bushy, dense growth; thick clusters of gold blooms; 2 ½ ft.; zones 7-9
		Vanhoutte Spirea	Diamond-shaped leaves; clusters of small, white blooms; 5 ft.; zones 4-8
FLOWERS		*Primula japonica (far left)*	Tubular, crimson flowers; pale green leaves; 2 ft.; zones 6-8
		Welsh Poppy *(left)*	Fern-shaped foliage; bright yellow or orange flowers; 18 in; zones 6-8
		King's Spear	Gray-green leaves; spikes of yellow flowers; 3 ft.; zones 6-9
		Mourning Widow	Bright green, lobed leaves; purplish maroon blooms; 30 in.; zones 4-9
BULBS		*Allium unifolium (far left)*	Carries one gray-green leaf; mauve-pink blooms; 1 ft.; zones 4-10
		Fritillaria *(left)*	Bell-shaped blooms in range of colors; 2-14 in.; zones 5-9
		Red Bell	Spikes of orange or red flowers flecked with yellow; 3 ft.; zones 6-9
		Yellow Mariposa	Three-petaled, yellow flowers with brown centers; 8 in.; zones 5-10
GROUNDCOVERS		Carpet Bugle *(far left)*	Purple foliage; short, blue flower spikes; 8 in.; zones 3-8
		Mountain Heather *(left)*	Evergreen; clusters of bell-shaped flowers; 8 in.; zones 2-5
		Crown Vetch	Deep pink blooms framed by Fern-like foliage; 18-24 in.; zones 5-7
		Snow-in-summer	Profusion of knitted, white blooms; silvery leaves; 9 in.; zones 4-7

TASKS & TECHNIQUES

A Basic Guide to
Planting Bulbs

Planting your bulbs in the right conditions will ensure a glorious show of colorful blooms.

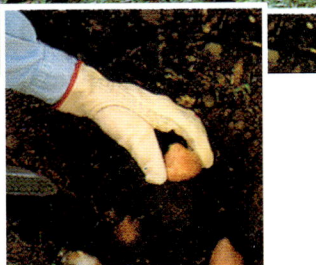

PLANTING A SHOW OF BULBS

YOU WILL NEED:

❏ Kneeling mat

❏ Garden spade, trowel, or bulb planting tool

❏ Plastic sheet

Tip

Create a dramatic effect by planting bulbs in large masses. Since bulbs are sold by color, you can choose vivid, contrasting colors, or more subtle combinations. Lay bulbs out on the ground before planting to get a sense of your color scheme.

1 **To plant a full bed** or wide border of bulbs, dig a trench, placing the soil on the side on a plastic sheet.

2 **Place bulbs** in trench according to your design. Plant close together for impact, but do not let them touch.

3 **Replace the soil,** being careful not to disturb the positioning of the bulbs. Firm soil once all bulbs are covered.

4 **Water thoroughly** if soil is dry, and then add a thick layer of mulch, such as pine bark, to keep bulbs moist.

PLANTING SINGLE BULBS

If you are planting a few bulbs or just one bulb in your garden, there is no need to dig out a tray bed. An easier way to plant a small number of bulbs is with a special bulb planting tool. Excellent bulbs for small plantings include:

● Emperor Tulips

● Irises

● Daffodils

● Crown Imperial Fritillaries

● Hyacinths

1 **Sink bulb planting tool** straight down into the soil. Pull up tool and squeeze its handle to remove soil plug.

2 **Place bulb** in the hole, making sure that it faces the right way up. Replace soil and water planting well.

Bulb Planting Basics

Bulbs let you create beautiful shows of multicolored blooms in stunning masses, and will flower year after year.

WHAT ARE BULBS?

Bulbs are "storage tanks". They help a plant to survive dormant periods, when it is too cold or hot for it to flower, and they nourish the plant during the growing and flowering season.

There are three major types of bulbs, including true bulbs, such as Hyacinths, Daffodils, and Tulips; tubers, such as Dahlias and some Begonias; and corms, such as Crocuses and Gladioli. All vary in shape as well as size.

Bulbs are sold when they are in a dormant state. You can order bulbs during the planting season from local garden centers and nurseries, or earlier from mail-order catalogs. Plant your bulbs as soon as possible to ensure that they grow.

Bulbs, such as these Irises, can make a spectacular border

HOW TO PLANT BULBS CORRECTLY

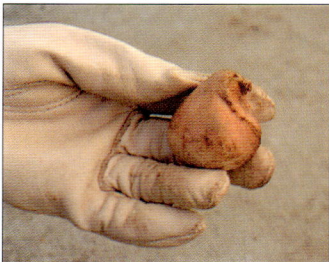

Teardrop-shaped bulbs, including large bulbs, such as Daffodils and Hyacinths, should be planted with their tips facing up. If their tips face down, they waste their energy trying to grow in the opposite direction.

Some bulbs, such as Irises, are flat or have "claws". If a bulb has an obviously flat side, plant this side facing up. Plant all bulbs that have appendages or roots facing down. If you are unsure, plant the bulb sideways.

BEST PLANTING DEPTHS

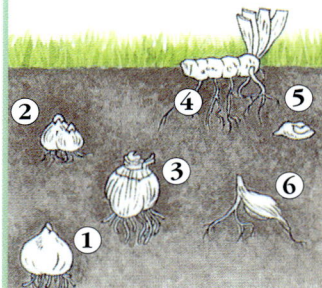

6-8 in.—Hyacinths
4-6 in.—Tulips (1)
3-4 in.—Gladioli, Fritillaries, Daffodils (3), Dahlias (6)
0-2 in.—Crocuses (2), Begonia tubers, Lilies, Ranunculus, Cyclamen, Anemones (5)
Surface—Iris rhizomes (4)

A Basic Guide to Planting Bulbs

Seasonal Tips

FALL
Planting bulbs for spring
Plant spring-flowering bulbs in the fall. Plant earlier in cold areas to avoid attack by frost.

SPRING
Planting bulbs for summer
Plant summer-flowering bulbs in a cool but frost-free place.

EARLY SUMMER
Cleaning up
Pinch the heads off faded flowers before they set seed. Let the leaves die naturally. Dig up spring-blooming bulbs (and some summer-blooming bulbs in cold climates) and store them in a dry, dark place for replanting the next year.

SUMMER
Planting bulbs for fall
Plant fall-flowering bulbs over the summer months.

Weather Watch

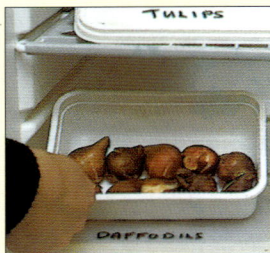

In warmer areas, give bulbs an artificial cold period to simulate winter. Place the bulbs in your refrigerator for about eight weeks to trick them into dormancy, so they can store energy for new growth. Keep fruit out of the refrigerator, as ripening fruit produces ethylene, a gas that will stop bulbs from flowering.

AFTERCARE

Cut faded blooms before the flowers have started to set seed. This will ensure that the bulb conserves and stores up all its energy, ready to produce new blooms in the next season.

Bulbs can be left in the ground. Some will, in time, spread out from their planting position and form new bulbs. This is called "naturalizing". After a few years, dig up and divide overcrowded bulbs.

Bulbs need to be dry. To store them, clean and keep them in a cool, dry place, such as a garage. Plant or replant them in well-drained soil. Dig in a gritty draining material, such as sand, if the soil is very wet.

A Guide to
Garden Wind Protection

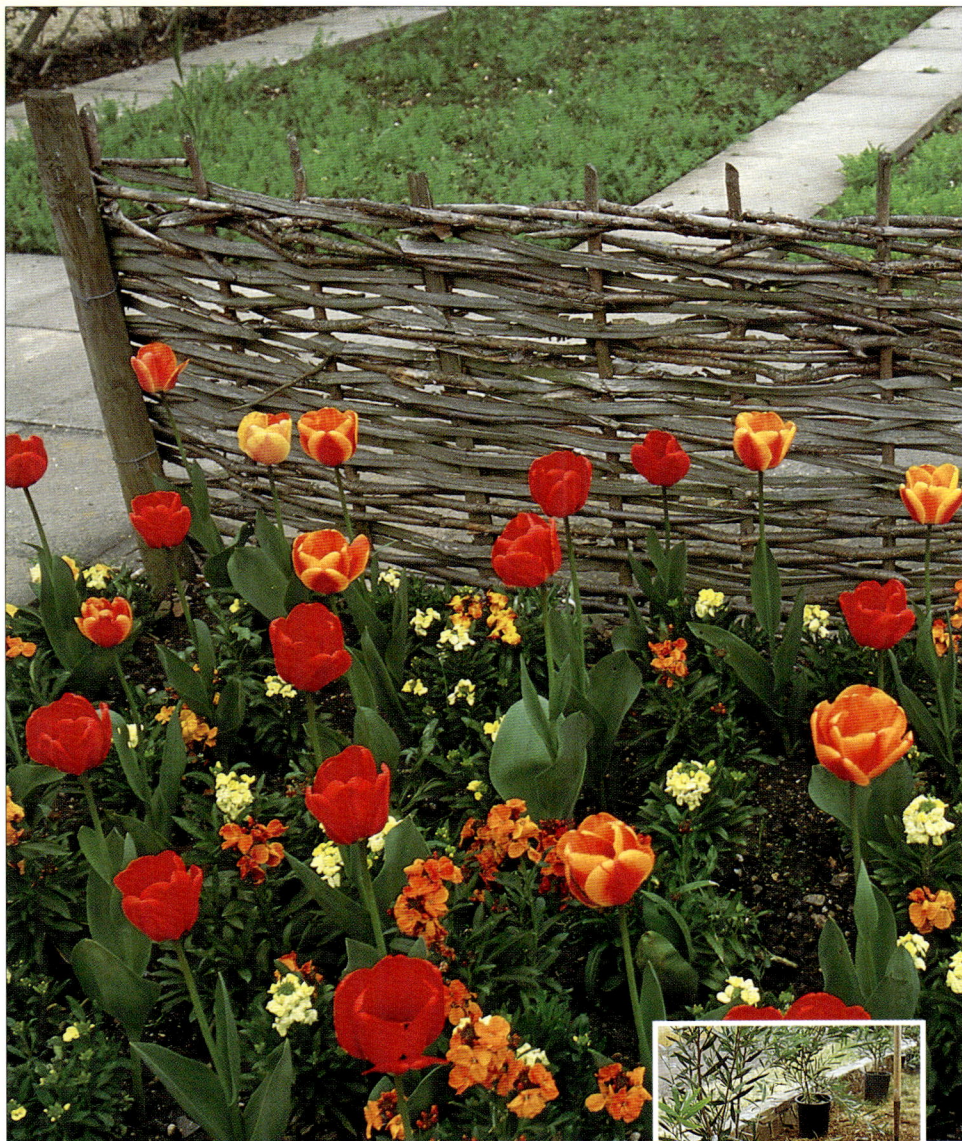

Tame the elements with proper plantings and structures to shield your landscape from wind.

CREATING A WINDBREAK: USING SHRUBS

YOU WILL NEED:

❑ Stakes
❑ Compost
❑ Shovel
❑ Six 5-gal. shrubs

1 **Determine the** prevailing wind direction. Lightly tap stakes into loose soil around garden, and see which ones are knocked down by the wind.

2 **Locate the windbreak** at right angles to the wind, 16-20 ft. behind the area to protect. Cultivate the soil, mixing in organic material.

3 **Set out plants,** placing them twice as close as normal plantings so that they will grow together to form an effective screen.

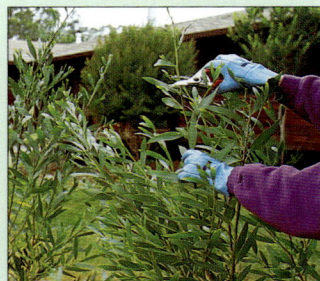

4 **Firm soil around plants** and water. Lightly prune foliage to give it a good shape, reduce stress from planting, and encourage bushiness.

CREATING A WINDBREAK: USING A STRUCTURE

YOU WILL NEED: ❑ 2 sturdy 8 ft. posts ❑ Concrete ❑ Lattice panel ❑ 3 Shrubs ❑ I Vine

1 **Choose area for screen.** Dig a 2 ft. hole for each post; set posts into concrete. Nail lattice panel to posts.

2 **Plant shrubs** a few feet behind the windward side of the screen to help reduce speed of wind hitting panel.

3 **Plant vine** on the garden side of the panel and intertwine the stems through the openings. Water well.

Sheltering Options

Help minimize wind problems in the garden with strategically placed plants, fences, or walls.

WHY PROTECT AGAINST WIND?

Very windy conditions can make your garden an unpleasant place for relaxing or working. Wind can cause damage to plants because it speeds moisture loss in both plant tissues and soil. In extreme cases, it can also tear foliage and snap large branches. Plants that have wilted from moisture loss are more susceptible to torn leaves, bent stems, and even broken limbs. Where winds blow daily or predictably, protection will help.

WHAT TO PROTECT

Plants most susceptible to wind damage are those with thin or brittle, weak stems and tender leaves or shallow roots. Young trees with thin trunks and rounded canopies are also in danger.

Newly installed plants are particularly vulnerable

Troubleshooter

Prevent damage from drying winds by mulching plants. A layer of compost will help keep soil from drying out during windy days.

Rows of plants work best to slow wind speed

until they have set out root systems to secure them and become established.

HOW TO PROTECT

Protection starts with prevention, especially if the site receives regular, strong winds. Choosing plants that tolerate, and even thrive, in windy areas will minimize trouble. Look for plants that take dry soil and have strong leaves and flexible stems.

Protect existing gardens with windbreaks in the form of hedges, rows of tall plants, or with structures, such as fences placed perpendicular to the prevailing winds.

Plant material has the advantage of density and height, which helps deflect and reduce wind speed. A row, or multiple rows, of plants gradually breaks the wind, providing shelter for the area beyond.

Fast-growing, deep-rooted, easily pruned shrubs and trees make the best windscreens. Positioned close together, they form an effective wind barrier.

Structures, including fences and supports, are another good solution. Fences and screens should be securely anchored and louvered or paneled to allow some air to pass through. For new plants, staked plastic sheets can provide some temporary shelter.

Installing a temporary screen

A Guide to Garden Wind Protection

Options for Wind Breaks

TYPE	WINDBREAK	DESCRIPTION
TREES	Shore Pine	Grows 30-40 ft. tall; space 15-20 ft. apart; bright green leaves, 1 ½-3 in. cones; evergreen; zones 6-8
	Poplar (*left*)	Fast-growing; grows to 80 ft. tall; space 10-15 ft. apart; oval, glossy leaves; deciduous; can be invasive; zones 3-9
	Box Elder	Fast-growing; grows to 50 ft. tall; space 12-15 ft. apart; light green or variegated leaves; deciduous; zones 3-9
SHRUBS	Privet	Grows 10-30 ft. tall; space 4-5 ft. apart; shiny, green leaves; white summer flowers; evergreen or deciduous; zones 6-10
	Portugal Laurel (*left*)	Adaptable; grows to 30 ft. tall; space 8-10 ft. apart; glossy foliage; small, white summer flowers; evergreen; zones 7-10
	Juniper	Slow-growing; 5-30 ft. tall; space 5-8 ft. apart; green or gray-green leaves; very hardy; evergreen; zones 3-9
STRUCTURES	Open-board fence	Provides good wind protection close to fence; use open-slot, vertical boards to let some air pass through
	Screen-block wall (*left*)	Uses masonry screen blocks with open pattern; attractive; good protection close to wall; works well as a low screen
	Chain-link fence	Provides some wind protection if covered with vigorous, leafy vines, such as English Ivy or deciduous Russian Vine

Seasonal Tips

SPRING
Planting & Installing
Plant or install new screens when ground thaws. Check to see that structures are well anchored. Prune evergreen shrubs; shape so the tops are narrower than the bottoms.

SUMMER
Watering
Water windbreak plants if rain is not plentiful. Most plants need the equivalent of 1 in. of rainfall each week, so soak the ground thoroughly when you water *(right)*. Cut any wayward stems to keep hedges neat.

WINTER
Pruning
Prune deciduous shrubs and trees while dormant, when the plants' branch structures are easy to see. Remove damaged branches, and trim to shape.

A Guide to
Growing Bulbs from Seeds

You can raise bushels of new bulbs with just a few simple seed-sowing techniques.

SOWING BULB SEEDS IN POTS

YOU WILL NEED:

- ❏ Clay or plastic pot
- ❏ Germinating mix
- ❏ Bulb seeds
- ❏ Fine gravel

Caution!

To prevent rot, it is important to drastically reduce watering when bulbs are not actively growing. Keep pots in a sheltered place where they will not be exposed to soaking rains. Once the leaves have yellowed and withered, water lightly every few weeks to keep soil from drying out.

1 Select a large plastic or clay pot and fill to within $1/2$ in. of the rim with a special, sterilized, germinating mix of potting soil.

2 Scatter seeds evenly over soil. Sprinkle a $1/8$ in. layer of germinating mix over seeds. Firm lightly. Cover with a $1/4$ in. layer of fine gravel.

3 Water to moisten potting soil thoroughly. Set the pot outdoors in a shady, protected spot and wait for sprouts to appear.

4 Water regularly while bulbs are actively growing. At the end of the second growing season, transplant seedlings to a larger pot.

GROWING BULB SEEDLINGS IN A NURSERY BED

Unlike most commercially available bulbs, seedling bulbs can be quite variable. If you would like to see your bulbs flower before you decide where to plant them, grow them in a special nursery bed until they reach flowering size. At that time, you can mark the color and flower forms you want to save and then transfer them to the garden once they have gone dormant.

1 To prepare a nursery bed, choose a sunny, well-drained site. An area that is 2-3 ft. square will give you plenty of room.

2 Loosen the soil, and then set the young bulbs 3-6 in. apart. Leave them undisturbed until they reach flowering size.

The Basics of Raising Bulbs

Fill your garden with beautiful bulbs without spending a fortune.

WHY GROW BULBS FROM SEEDS?

There is nothing like a showy sweep of bulbs for brightening the spring garden, but it can cost quite a bit of money to buy enough bulbs to make a worthwhile display. With a minimal outlay and a little patience, however, you can have as many bulbs as you want by growing them from seeds. Some bulbs naturally produce seedlings that all

Seed-grown bulbs often bloom in a range of colors

look very similar; others, especially seedlings grown from hybrid varieties, will naturally produce a range of colors and flower forms.

WHEN TO SOW

You will get the best results by sowing seeds when they are fresh. Seeds of spring-flowering bulbs usually ripen by mid-summer; summer-flowering bulbs produce seeds in late summer to fall. If you sow fresh seeds in summer or fall, they will usually sprout early the next spring. You can expect bulbs to reach flowering size three to five years after sowing.

HOW TO CARE FOR SEEDLINGS

Place newly sown pots of seeds in a cold frame or a sheltered spot outdoors. Once seeds have sprouted,

keep them evenly moist until their foliage withers and dies; after that, water sparingly. When new growth appears or when fall arrives— whichever comes first— begin watering and feeding the bulbs regularly. Keep the soil moist until top growth dies down again. At this time, move bulbs to garden, or transfer them to a pot of fresh potting soil and grow them for another year before planting them in the ground.

Keep pots in a sheltered spot

Tip

Since bulbs tend to be fairly small, especially for the first few years, there is no need to give them individual pots. A 4 in. pot can easily hold a dozen seedlings or about six two- to three-year-old bulbs. When large bulbs are big enough for the garden, remove from their pot and space out as you would purchased bulbs. Small bulbs are even easier to plant; simply slide the mass of soil and bulbs out of the pot and plant the whole clump in the garden.

A Guide to Growing Bulbs from Seeds

Easy-to-grow Bulbs from Seeds

SIZE	NAME	DESCRIPTION	COMMENTS
SMALL BULBS	Spanish Bluebell	Clusters of nodding, bell-shaped spring flowers in pink, blue, or white on 12 in. stems	Plant in clumps in beds and borders, or naturalize in groundcovers or woodlands
	Crocus *(left)*	Silky-petalled, goblet-shaped spring flowers to 4 in. tall in white, yellow, or purple	Ideal for containers and gardens; mice love bulbs, so protect pots of seedlings
	Squill	Nodding, star-shaped early spring flowers on 4-6 in. stems in light or deep blue	Use in containers, borders, beds, or lawns; can reseed in garden to form large clumps
	Grape Hyacinth *(left)*	Grape-like clusters of small, globular, purple flowers on 6 in. stems in spring	Good under trees and shrubs or naturalized in grass; look best planted in large masses
LARGE BULBS	Daffodil *(left)*	Spring trumpets in yellow, white, pink, orange, or bicolors on stems to 18 in.	Plant just about anywhere in garden; propagate especially nice seedlings by division
	Lily	Large, trumpet- or star-shaped summer flowers in a range of colors on stems up to 5 ft. tall	Take up to five years to bloom from seeds; good for borders and cutting
	Tulip *(left)*	Showy, cup-shaped spring flowers in a rainbow of colors on 6-30 in. stems	Seedlings from hybrids often differ from parents; species Tulips tend to look the same

Seasonal Tips

EARLY SPRING
Repotting

If bulb seedlings are growing very vigorously during their second season of growth, slide the mass out of pot and plant the whole thing in a larger pot to give bulbs more room.

SUMMER
Gathering seeds

Most bulbs bear seeds in swollen capsules atop the old flowering stems *(right)*; a few, like Crocuses, produce seeds at ground level. Watch capsules carefully and gather seeds as capsules start to split. Sow seeds as soon as possible after collecting them.

EARLY FALL
Planting

The best time to move young bulbs to the garden is while they are resting or just as they are beginning to produce new growth. Transplant smaller bulbs in clumps; plant larger bulbs individually.

A Basic Guide to
Dividing Bulbs

Allow your garden's flower bulbs to supply you with more of a good thing for free.

Multiplying Beauty

Increase your stock of flower bulbs by going to the source.

WHAT IS DIVISION?

Most flower bulbs regularly produce immature growths called bulblets. Division is the process by which these growths are separated from the older parent bulbs, and then replanted in the garden to grow new plants.

The three basic types of bulbs that are divided are the typical pear-shaped "true" bulbs, such as Tulips; bulbs with layered scales, such as Lilies; and corms, such as Crocuses, which resemble bulbs, but are more solid and swollen, and produce offsets called "cormels".

Did You Know?

Hyacinths can be stimulated to grow small bulbs. Dig up a Hyacinth bulb after its foliage fades in spring. With a knife, score an "X" along the bulb's bottom and store it in moist sand or loose soil in a warm, dark, moist place until small bulbs grow on the cuts. Plant bulb with the small bulbs pointing up and divide into individual bulbs at the end of the growing season.

Plant bulblets near larger bulbs to easily locate for digging up

WHY DIVIDE BULBS?

Division not only provides free bulbs, it also lets existing bulbs grow stronger. Bulbs spend a good deal of energy supporting a bulblet. When the smaller growth is removed, the parent bulb has more energy for blooming, resulting in bigger flowers.

WHEN TO DIVIDE

Spring-flowering bulbs, such as Daffodils, need time to regenerate after flowering, so wait until foliage begins to yellow before dividing them. After summer-flowering bulbs such as Lilies bloom, wait a few weeks, allowing them to rest before you divide. Summer-flowering bulbs that are not very hardy, such as Dahlias, should be dug up in fall and stored indoors until spring, when they can be divided and replanted in the garden.

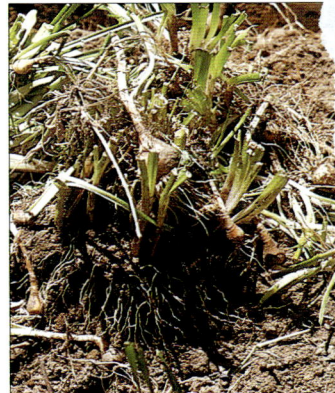

Daffodils dug up to be divided

HOW TO DIVIDE

Division is simply stripping new growths off the parent bulb and either planting or storing them to plant later. Prevent small bulblets from blooming the first year by nipping off flowers. This will prevent them from wasting their energy trying to grow blooms, and will allow them to grow large enough to put on a big display.

DIVIDING SIMPLE BULBS

YOU WILL NEED:

- ❏ Large Daffodil bulb
- ❏ Garden fork
- ❏ Bulb booster
- ❏ Trowel
- ❏ Compost

Troubleshooter

Root and stem rot are two of the most common causes of bulb failure. To avoid this, always plant in a well-drained location and store bulbs in a moist, but not soggy, environment. Dusting bulblets with a fungicide will also help you avoid these fungal diseases.

1 **Dig up the Daffodil** bulb. It should be healthy, large, and not showing any signs of mold. Inspect the bulb, checking for bulblets growing on its side.

2 **With your fingers**, pull off any bulblets from the original Daffodil bulb. Remove them slowly and carefully to avoid injuring the parent bulb.

3 **Replant the Daffodil** bulblets, mixing a trowel of bulb booster into soil at the bottom of the hole. Plant these bulblets twice as deep as normal.

4 **Mulch the planting area** with a 2-3 in. layer of compost. Fertilize planting in spring with bulb booster just as new growth appears.

DIVIDING SCALY BULBS

YOU WILL NEED: ❏ Lily bulb ❏ Fork ❏ Fungicide ❏ Hormone powder ❏ Vermiculite

1 **Dig up a large Lily bulb** after its foliage has turned completely yellow. You can cut off the tops at this time.

2 **Peel off** the outermost scales of the Lily bulb. Dust scales with a fungicide, such as captan, and hormone powder.

3 **Store the scales** in moist vermiculite in a paper bag. Place in cool place until roots begin to grow. Plant in spring.

A Basic Guide to Dividing Bulbs

Best Bulbs for Dividing

PLANT	WHEN TO DIVIDE	DIVISION TIPS
Tulip (*left*)	Late spring after the foliage has almost, but not completely, died down	Pull small bulblets from base of bulb; hybrid Tulips are usually unsuitable for dividing
Daffodil	Late spring after the foliage has almost, but not completely, died down	Dig up and divide every few years as the number and size of blooms decreases
Crocus (*left*)	Spring; lift Crocus corms as soon as their foliage starts to die down	Small cormels are difficult to divide individually, so separate foliage clumps instead
Lily	Late summer as foliage dies back; only divide when plants are overcrowded	Lilies should be undisturbed for years; on large bulb, you can peel off the outer two scaly layers
Hyacinth (*left*)	Spring, after foliage is almost, but not completely, gone from the plant	Cutting bulb causes it to grow small bulbs at its base; divide only overcrowded plants
Allium	Early fall, after the foliage almost completely dies and plants can be lifted	Bulblets form rapidly on mature bulbs, so space farther apart to give them room to grow
Gladiolus	Lift in early fall after stalks and blooms die; store until spring and then divide	Mature bulblets will almost fall off the Gladioli bulb as you dig up the parent plant
Scilla (*left*)	Late summer, after the plant's foliage has almost completely died back	Wait until overcrowded and then carefully remove largest bulblets from the parent and replant
Snowdrops	Early spring, after blooms die, but before the foliage begins dying	After four to five years, break foliage clumps into three or four pieces and then replant

Seasonal Tips

SPRING/SUMMER
Dividing
Divide summer-flowering bulbs in spring and plant bulblets in garden (*right*). After foliage yellows in summer, dig up and divide spring-flowering bulbs.

FALL
Preparing for winter
Remove tender bulbs and store them in a cool, dark place for the winter. Divide tender corms, such as Gladioli, and store until they can be replanted in spring.

PLANT GUIDE

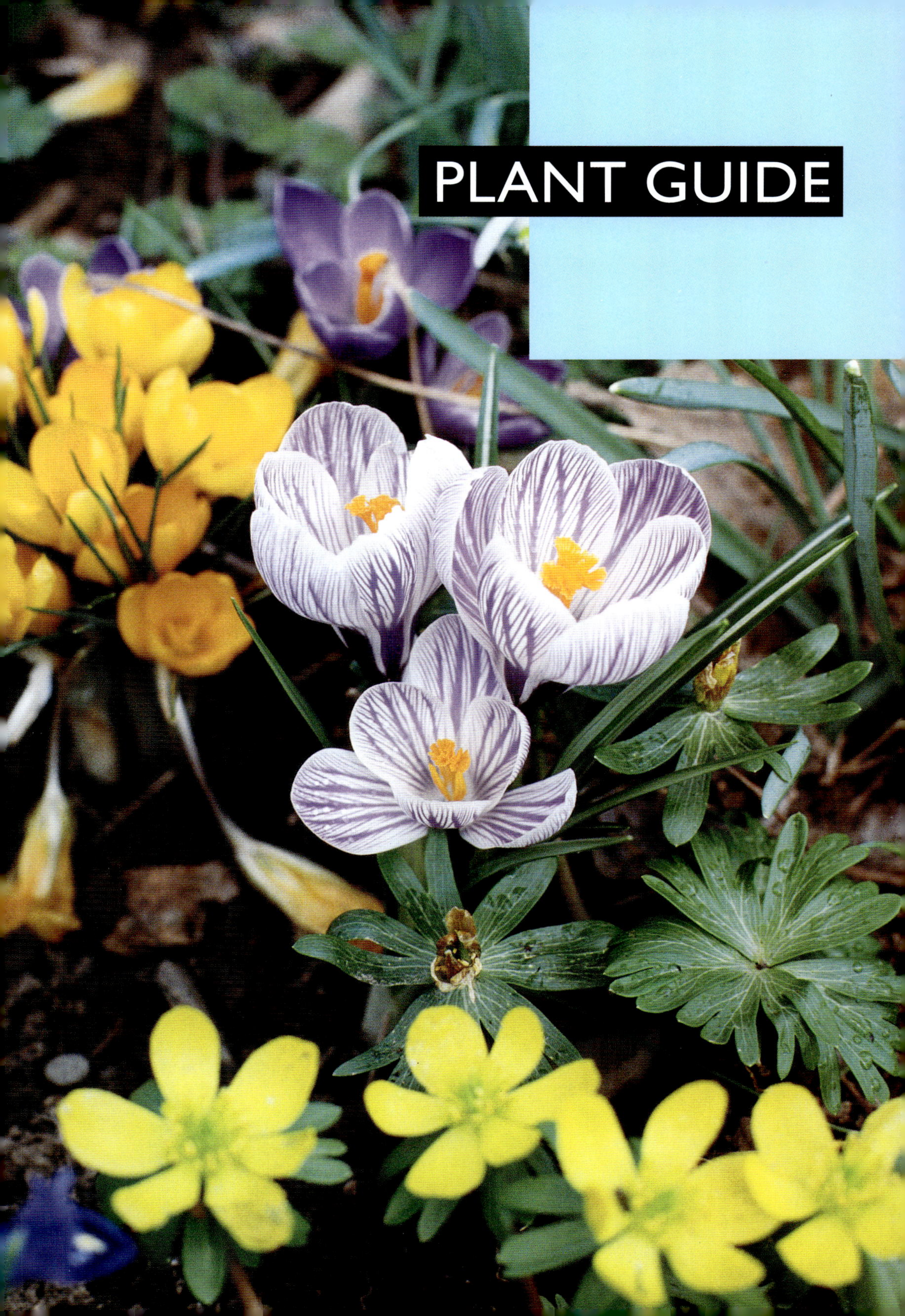

Bearded Irises

Brightly colored petals with a twist

Season	Special Features	Best Conditions	
✳ **Flowers early to late spring**	✓ **Easy care** ✂ **Good for cut flowers**	🌐 **Zones 3-9** ☀ **Full sun** 🔱 **Well-drained soil**	Height: 4-36 in. Spread: 4-24 in.

over a bed of Lamb's-ears

Bearded Iris 'Going My Way'

PLANTING & AFTERCARE

YOU WILL NEED: ❏ Bearded Iris bulbs (rhizomes) ❏ Spade or garden trowel ❏ Compost ❏ Bone meal

1 **Dig up the soil** in your planting area 6-8 in. deep. Add one cup of well-rotted compost and one cup of bone meal per square foot of soil.

2 **Plant the rhizomes** horizontally, with leaves face-up and roots face-down. Never plant rhizomes deeper than 1 in. or they may rot.

3 **Add soil,** leaving the top one-third of the rhizome showing. Point the fan of leaves in the direction you want the Irises to grow.

4 **Water thoroughly** after planting all of your Irises. Do not mulch over the rhizomes or you may prevent them from growing.

5 **Apply an all-purpose** organic fertilizer, such as bone meal, at half-rate to the Irises in early spring. Sprinkle it around the rhizomes.

Dollar Sense

Every three to five years, cut the rhizome in two or more pieces so that each has a small fan of leaves and some roots. Replant the sections.

Lavish Color Combinations

Bearded Irises provide stunning color and long-lasting cut flowers for any spring garden.

COLORS & VARIETIES

Bearded Irises are considered the most elegant of all Irises. They are distinguished by their "beards", which are distinctive rows of colored hair along the center of their downturned petals.

These spring bloomers range from 4-6 in. dwarfs to varieties that grow over 3 ft. tall. 'Superstition' is a dramatic variety, growing over 3 ft. tall, and producing full, nearly black flowers. At the other end of the color spectrum, 'Cotton Blossom' offers frilly, pristine white flowers. For luscious salmon hues, try 'Bright Vision'.

The gold 'Honey Glazed'

Irises and Daisies by a fence

WHERE TO PLANT

Bearded Irises make for a strong display of color and form, whether planted by themselves or mixed in a flower border. These elegant blooms are often grown in spring beds or borders.

Splash some color in a rock garden with a dwarf Bearded Iris, such as the red, 7 in. tall 'Promise'.

Perk up a shrub border by planting several Bearded Iris varieties in front of it. Fill out a border of Lilacs with a mass planting of 'Cabaret Royale', a Bearded Iris with dark purple lower petals, lavender upper petals, and a bright gold beard.

A cut-flower garden is a traditional location for Bearded Irises. The amazing diversity of colors available makes it easy to create a personalized color scheme. Space rows 24-36 in. apart for ease of cutting.

PERFECT PARTNERS

Grouped together in plantings of 15 or more, Irises add powerful beauty to any flower bed or border. Combine with flowers whose shades are strong enough to compete with Iris colors.

Mix early-blooming dwarf Bearded Irises with Daffodils and Tulips for an impressive display of early

Violet Bearded Irises towering

spring color. The yellow Iris, 'Canary Prince', is handsome planted next to 'Red Riding Hood' Tulips and purple 'Enchantress' Crocuses.

Low-growing, silver foliage plants, such as Lamb's-ears, are attractive as an edging in front of Bearded Irises. Combine the silver with the deep red of 'Play with Fire', the burgundy 'Chippendale', or the delicate deep pink of 'Far Corners'.

Peonies often share the same bloom time as Irises. Their deep green foliage and billowy blooms will set off the vibrant hues of the Iris.

Secrets of Success

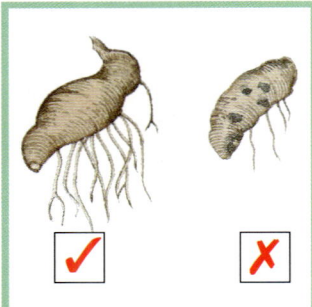

BUYING HINTS

- **Buy firm and plump** rhizomes. Look for those with stringy roots that are all about the same length.
- **Avoid rhizomes** that are soft to the touch. Do not buy those that show signs of mold or mildew, such as black or gray spots.

SUN & SOIL

- **Full sun.** Bearded Irises need at least a half day of sun, but their color will be more vibrant if they receive a full day of direct sun.
- **Well-drained soil.** If the soil drains poorly, improve drainage by digging in a thick layer of compost.

SPECIAL ADVICE

- **Never apply fertilizer** directly to the rhizome, as the fertilizer can burn it.
- **After they bloom,** cut off the entire flowering stem, leaving just the fan of leaves. The leaves will help build up the rhizome's food storage for the winter.

Seasonal Tips

SPRING— EARLY SUMMER
Ordering & Planting
Order Bearded Irises from bulb catalogs now, so that they will arrive in time for fall planting. Plant Bearded Iris rhizomes in warmer areas, such as zones 8-9.

LATE SUMMER— EARLY FALL
Dividing
Divide older Bearded Iris rhizomes. Cut away woody sections of rhizome and replant remaining sections.

FALL
Cleaning up & Planting
Trim back foliage to within 4-5 in. of the rhizomes. Remove any shriveled or dead leaves (below). Plant new Iris rhizomes in colder areas.

Plant Doctor

Iris borers are pink larvae that feed on Iris leaves and rhizomes. A thorough clean-up in late fall will remove most of their eggs. After Irises flower, dig up infested rhizomes and cut out borers. Dust rhizomes with sulfur and replant.

Crested Irises

Lush spikes of green studded with frilly blooms

Season	Special Features	Best Conditions	
❋ Flowers in spring	✓ Easy to grow ≋ Good groundcover	🌐 Zones 4-10 ☀ Full sun to partial shade 🔨 Moist, well-drained soil	Height: 4-24 in. ◄ Spread: 6-12 in.

A Sea of Soft Blooms

Vigorous Crested Irises offer evergreen leaves topped by spectacular spring flowers.

COLORS & VARIETIES

Crested Irises have a frilly crest on their lower petals. The blooms resemble a cross between Bearded Irises and Orchids. They quickly spread by runners to cover large areas and have evergreen fans of sword-shaped foliage. The various species vary in size and hardiness.

The Dwarf Crested Iris *(Iris cristata)* is only 4-6 in. tall and does well in cool, moist soil in partial shade in zones 4-8. The dainty blooms are usually a soft lavender-blue with yellow crests, but there is a white form, 'Alba'.

Roof Iris *(I. tectorum)* is more tender (recommended for zones 6-10), but it is also more drought tolerant and takes either full sun or partial shade. The ruffled blooms on 12 in. stems are rich blue with white crests, or white with yellow crests in 'Alba'.

Orchid Iris *(I. japonica)* is best for moist, humid areas

At the base of a stone wall

in zones 9-10, where it flowers from spring well into summer. 'Nada' is a vigorous grower with ruffled, white blooms speckled in orange.

WHERE TO PLANT

Crested Irises will fill low-maintenance borders and beds in sun or partial shade with elegant foliage and long-lasting, colorful blooms.

As an interesting alternative to overused groundcovers, Crested Irises can be naturalized under tall trees or among shrubs. When in bloom, they make a breathtaking sight.

Use a ribbon of Crested Irises to unify a perennial bed, providing an edge that remains attractive year-round in warm winter regions. Confine their spreading runners with an edging strip.

A moist pocket in a rock garden displays the smaller species beautifully. Their pale blooms shine against a neutral backdrop of stone.

Dainty Dwarf Crested Irises

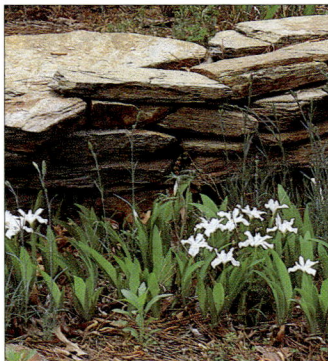

Lovely with Trilliums, Wild Blu

A container of Crested Irises will bloom over a long period. Container planting both confines the spreading roots and allows for easy protection from severe winter weather.

PERFECT PARTNERS

The small, delicate blooms of Crested Irises show best against a quiet backdrop. Contrast their spiky foliage with soft, Fern-like plants or bold, rounded leaves.

The silvery blue blooms of 'Pal-tec' Roof Iris unfurl at the same time as pink spikes of 'Perfecta' Bergenias. The glossy, heart-shaped Bergenia leaves make a perfect year-round foil for the Iris.

Plant round-leaved, evergreen European Ginger as a shiny, green backdrop to

Phlox, and Wild Columbines

the pastel blooms of tiny Dwarf Crested Irises. White-flowered 'Alba' is especially showy in the shade.

Variegated leaves and white blooms of 'Kamayana' Orchid Irises make a strong impression with 'Taylortown Red' Verbenas, which cover evergreen foliage with scarlet blooms from spring to fall.

'Alba' Dwarf Crested Irises

PLANTING & AFTERCARE

YOU WILL NEED: ❑ Bareroot Crested Iris plants ❑ Shovel ❑ Trowel ❑ Compost or leaf mold ❑ Mulch

1 Plant Crested Irises in early to mid-fall. Loosen soil to a depth of 6 in. and work in abundant amounts of compost or leaf mold.

2 Space Dwarf Crested Irises 4 in., Roof Irises 8 in., and Orchid Irises 15 in. apart. Set rhizomes on top of soil with leaves pointing up.

3 Gently firm roots into soil, but do not cover or they will rot. Water well and mulch (keep off roots) to prevent frost heaving.

4 Keep soil moist year round. Loosen soil around Irises to encourage their spread. Insert a barrier to prevent spreading.

5 Deadhead spent flowers to neaten plants and prevent seed formation, which weakens plants. Cut off any yellowed leaves.

Tip

Crested Irises soon become too crowded to bloom well. Thin in early fall by cutting off runners. Replant immediately.

Secrets of Success

BUYING HINTS

● **Buy bareroot plants** with healthy, green foliage fans and firm rhizomes that appear freshly dug.
● **Avoid plants** without leaves or with soft, limp rhizomes. Do not buy any Irises that have mushy, discolored leaves.

SUN & SOIL

● **Full sun** to partial shade. In hot climates, some shade helps keep soil cooler. Full sun is ideal in cooler areas.
● **Moist,** well-drained soil. Crested Irises look their best if soil never becomes dry, but they do not tolerate soggy, poorly drained soils.

SPECIAL ADVICE

● **Crested Irises** prefer soil that is loose and humus-rich. Frequently cultivate soil and sprinkle with compost or leaf mold.
● **If a late frost** nips early flower stalks on your Irises, cut them back. They will usually recover.

Seasonal Tips

EARLY FALL
Thinning & Planting
Plant new divisions of Crested Irises as soon as the weather has cooled. Dig up or pull up runners from crowded plantings and cut off; replant right away in prepared soil.

MID-SPRING—SUMMER
Deadheading
Remove spent blooms to prevent seeds from forming. Cut Orchid Irises freely for indoor bouquets to encourage reblooming.

SUMMER
Maintaining
Water deeply whenever the soil becomes dry. Topdress plantings with a thin layer of compost or leaf mold. Remove any leaves that turn yellow (below) to encourage fresh leaves to grow.

Plant Doctor

The only disease that troubles Crested Irises is bacterial soft rot. The first sign is yellowing of the leaf tip, followed by a softening of the roots. Remove any infected leaves and roots, and dust the entire planting with powdered sulfur. If soil drains poorly, raise beds.

Crocuses

Electric blooms to melt the last traces of winter

Season	Special Features	Best Conditions	
✹ Flowers late winter to spring Some varieties: flower in fall	✓ Easy to grow 🕷 Disease resistant	🌐 Zones 3-8 ☀ Full sun or light shade 🔨 Well-drained soil	Height: 3-8 in. ↕ ← Spread: 2-4 in.

and 'Flower Record' Crocuses

C. chrysanthus 'Snow Bunting'

PLANTING & AFTERCARE

YOU WILL NEED: ❑ Crocus bulbs ❑ Trowel
❑ Compost ❑ Bone meal ❑ Shredded pine bark

1 **In early fall,** dig a hole about 5 in. deep, and wide enough for all your bulbs. Add compost and bone meal, using 1 cup of each per square foot.

2 **Add 2 in. of soil** and mix well with both the compost and bone meal. Firmly place bulbs in soil, pointed ends up, 2 in. apart.

3 **Cover the bulbs with** remaining soil. Tamp soil down firmly using the palms of your hands. Do not overly compact the soil.

4 **Water well.** Once the ground freezes, add 2 in. of shredded pine bark to conserve moisture and keep the bulbs' temperature stable.

Tip

Splash some color across your lawn by planting Crocuses under the turf. Dig up a small chunk of lawn to below the roots. Sprinkle in bone meal, place bulbs tip up, and then replace turf. Do not mow until foliage dies completely to ensure that they bloom the following year.

Pleasing Bursts of Color

Crocuses provide the first flowers of spring in cheery shades of blue, yellow, and white.

COLORS & VARIETIES

Crocuses are simple and colorful flowers. They are available in a medley of designs, ranging from solid colors to stripes. Each flower contains a simple cluster of petals above a short stem surrounded by green or variegated spiky foliage.

There are two basic Crocus types: wild species and common Dutch hybrids. Wild species are the small varieties, featuring up to twenty blooms from a single bulb, and are known for their unusual color blends. The species *C. chrysanthus* includes such vibrant varieties as 'Blue Bird', with sky blue, white-edged petals and deep orange centers. For striking, bright white petals, try 'Snow Bunting'.

Common Crocuses are generally larger, producing up to six flowers per bulb and blooming a week or so

'Dutch Yellow' Crocus

later than wild species. 'Grand Maitre' is a well-known common variety with dramatic lavender petals.

WHERE TO PLANT

As the first flowers to rise in spring, Crocuses look good just about anywhere. Plant them in your lawn and other unusual settings.

Wake up your rock garden with a crowd of Crocuses. Their small size and knife-like foliage will look stunning surrounding small rocks or nestled between larger stones.

Create an exciting early spring flower bed by planting a multicolored row of bright Crocuses in front of your evergreen shrubs. The green will serve as a lush backdrop for the cheery and vibrant Crocus colors.

Plant Crocus bulbs in a perennial bed for color in stages. The early-blooming Crocus flowers will give way to a burst of perennial blooms later in the season.

C. sativus 'Saffron Crocus'

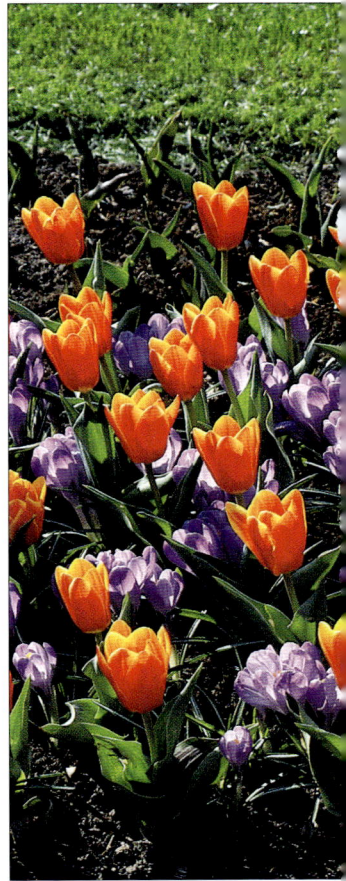

A bed of 'Princess Irene' Tulips

PERFECT PARTNERS

Crocuses look their best when paired with flowers in similar or stronger shades.

Plant them with other early bloomers, such as *Iris reticulata* and Snowdrops, for a rainbow-colored display.

Group Crocuses near the base of early spring-blooming shrubs. With orange-yellow petals dotted in bronze, 'Canarybird' will harmonize with the yellow-flowered Mahonia. Gleaming white 'Jeanne d'Arc' shines when planted beneath 'Loderi's' pendulous clusters of pale pink to white flowers.

Secrets of Success

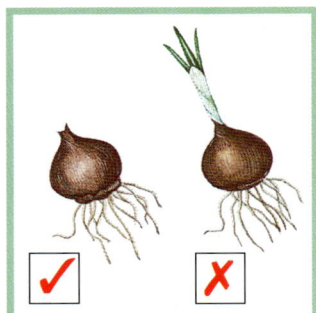

BUYING HINTS

● **Buy firm,** plump bulbs in late summer or early fall. If you purchase prepackaged Crocus bulbs, feel each one to ensure its firmness.
● **Avoid bulbs** that are at all soft to the touch. Discard those with spots or signs of growth, such as a green tail.

SUN & SOIL

● **Full sun or partial** shade. Crocuses will grow well in the dappled shade of a tree growing new leaves.
● **Well-drained soil.** When planting in poorly drained soil, dig several inches of compost into the soil to improve drainage.

SPECIAL ADVICE

● **The foliage of a Crocus** needs to ripen and die naturally for the bulb to come back the next year, so do not cut the foliage.
● **For a carnival of color,** plant several Crocus varieties in natural bouquets of 25 or more bulbs.

Seasonal Tips

SUMMER
Ordering
Order bulbs from catalogs as early as possible to receive Crocuses at planting time.

EARLY FALL
Planting
Spring-blooming bulbs can be planted up until first frost, but smaller bulbs do best if they have time to adjust before the ground freezes.

EARLY WINTER
Mulching
Once the ground has frozen, cover the planting area with several inches of mulch to provide thermal insulation.

SPRING
Fertilizing
Remove mulch as bulbs begin to emerge. Apply bone meal as the flowers fade (*below*).

Plant Doctor

Squirrels and many other rodents love to eat newly planted Crocuses. Prevent damage by covering the planting trench with screen or chicken wire. Remove the protection in early spring, or emerging growth may be stunted.

Dutch Hyacinths

A crayon-box assortment of vibrant blooms

Season	Special Features	Best Conditions
✻ Flowers in early spring	❧ Fragrant ✂ Good for cutting	⊕ Zones 3-8 ☀ Full sun ⚒ Fertile, well-drained soil

Height: 6-12 in.

Spread: 4-8 in.

f spring-flowering bulbs

'Pink Pearl' with yellow Tulips

PLANTING & AFTERCARE

YOU WILL NEED: ❏ Hyacinth bulbs ❏ Chicken wire ❏ Compost ❏ Bone meal ❏ Mulch ❏ Fertilizer

1 Dig a large, round trench 6 in. deep, in early fall. Line the bottom and sides of the hole with chicken wire to protect against gophers.

2 Add one trowel of compost and one of bone meal per square foot of planting hole. Place bulbs tip up, 6-8 in. apart.

3 Fill the hole with soil, being careful not to move the bulbs. Firm soil down with your hands. Water and mulch with shredded pine bark.

4 Fertilize after the Dutch Hyacinth's foliage begins to develop and grow. Spray the foliage with liquid plant food, such as fish emulsion.

5 Stake the flower spikes if they show signs of leaning. Leave foliage intact and let it completely die before removing.

Tip

Hyacinths are ideal for growing indoors. Plant in a shallow, insulated pot in fall, leave outside for ten weeks, and bring inside for winter blooms.

Scented Towers of Color

No early spring garden should be without a planting of these regal, upright flowers.

COLORS & VARIETIES

Dutch Hyacinths are classic flower bulbs with spikes of waxy, bell-shaped blooms growing from the center of long, narrow leaf clusters. Hyacinths offer pure shades of pink, purple, red, cream, salmon, and even sky blue.

'Distinction' bears flower spikes of an unusual, dusty maroon color, making it an excellent choice for a subdued color scheme. For the most fragrant Dutch Hyacinth, try the deep rosy pink 'Pink Pearl', or select 'Delft Blue' for the signature Holland blue color on large, towering flower spikes.

WHERE TO PLANT

Their stiff, upright growth makes Dutch Hyacinths perfect for mass plantings in curving sweeps of color, or as smaller groups of color in shallow containers.

'Blue Surprise' Hyacinths

The sugary pink 'Lady Derby'

Use these flower bulbs under a spring-flowering tree to draw attention to its budding display. They also add texture and fragrance.

In a terra-cotta pot, Hyacinths provide exuberant color and perfume near the front door or on a patio.

A cluster of Dutch Hyacinths in a range of colors adds a formal accent at the corner of a Boxwood hedge or other neatly clipped evergreen hedge.

PERFECT PARTNERS

The best companions for Dutch Hyacinths are other colorful, spring-blooming bulbs, trees, and shrubs.

Flowering Cherry and Plum trees bloom at the same time as Dutch Hyacinths. The pink or white blooms on the trees will enhance the deep violet hues of enchanting 'Crystal Palace' Dutch Hyacinths and the stately blue of 'Peter Stuyvesant'.

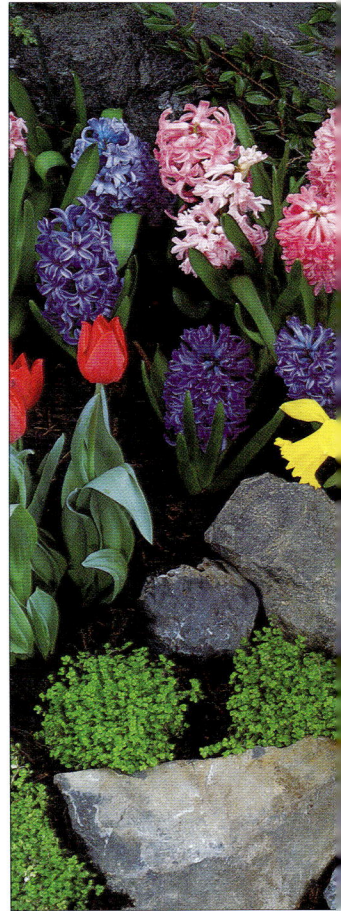

Dutch Hyacinths in a garden

Tulips have the same upright growth as Hyacinths, and early-season varieties bloom at the same time and in compatible colors. Pair lemon yellow Tulips with the unique, rich salmon 'Gipsy Queen' or the stunning scarlet of 'Red Rocket'.

Star Magnolias bloom just in time to accompany the richly hued spires of Dutch Hyacinths planted at their feet. Combine Magnolias in shades of pink and red with the baby pink of 'Anna Marie', the lilac-colored 'Amethyst', and the creamy white blooms of 'Carnegie'.

Secrets of Success

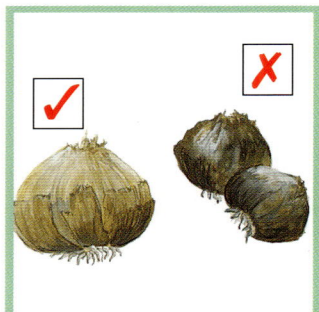

BUYING HINTS

- **Buy the largest** Dutch Hyacinth bulbs you can find in fall. The bigger the bulb, the bigger the flowers.
- **Avoid soft, bruised,** or moldy bulbs. Do not buy Dutch Hyacinth bulbs that have long, curling growth showing from the tip.

SUN & SOIL

- **Four hours of sun.** Exposure to full sun ensures stiff, upright flower spikes, but Dutch Hyacinths will also bloom in partial shade.
- **Well-drained soil.** The more fertile the soil, the more years the bulbs will return and bloom.

SPECIAL ADVICE

- **Dutch Hyacinth** flowers are smaller in successive years, so plant new bulbs every two to three years for the best floral display.
- **An attractive** and inexpensive way to stake Hyacinths is with forked branches cut from shrubs.

Seasonal Tips

FALL
Planting

Buy and plant bulbs. If your area experiences cold winters, plant early in the season so that bulbs have a chance to grow roots. The hotter the climate, the later you plant, so in warm areas, store bulbs in a cold place until you plant in late fall.

SPRING
Feeding

Fertilize Hyacinths with a liquid plant food just before they bloom to encourage the largest flowers the next year.

LATE SPRING
Cutting

Remove spent flower spikes *(below)* before they wilt, and continue watering yellowing foliage. Do not cut ripening foliage or bulb may not flower the following year.

Plant Doctor

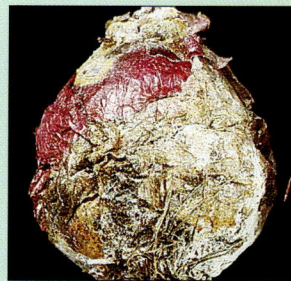

Poorly developing plants and decaying bulbs with black streaks on their base are signs of bulb rot. This fungal disease causes bulbs to degenerate and often die. Throw out infested bulbs and do not plant in this area.

Fritillaries

Exquisite, bell-shaped blooms to ring in spring

Season	Special Features	Best Conditions	
✹ Flowers in spring	✓ Easy care 🕷 Disease resistant	🌐 Zones 3-8 ☀ Full sun to partial shade 🔧 Rich, well-drained soil	↕ Height: 9-36 in. ← Spread: 3-8 in. →

Versatile Nodding Bells

From modest Checkered Lilies to stately Crown Imperials, Fritillaries enhance any garden.

COLORS & VARIETIES

The pendant, bell-shaped blooms of Fritillaries are elegant additions to the spring garden. Fritillaries are available in colors from pure white to checkered mauve, and in sizes ranging from just a few inches to several feet.

Among the tallest Fritillaries, Crown Imperials *(Fritillaria imperialis)* sport clusters of showy, yellow or orange blooms on 2-3 ft. stems, crowned with tufts of leaves. 'Rubra Maxima' is a popular red-orange variety.

Checkered Lilies *(F. meleagris)*, with dainty bells held singly on 8-12 in. stems, are more understated. They flower in white, mauve, and maroon, quaintly marked with checkers. 'Alba' is a pure white form.

There are also lovely, less-familiar species, such as the very hardy yellow *F. pallidiflora*, which will bloom in zone 2, and the exotic Persian Fritillary, with purple bells on 3 ft. stems.

Crown Imperial 'Aurea'

WHERE TO PLANT

With such a wide range of choices, there is a Fritillary suited to just about any garden situation, from a sunny border in your garden to a quiet, shady corner of your backyard.

Crown Imperials do best in sunny flower beds. They will bloom successfully in moist soil that is rich in organic matter and in a site where they can flower undisturbed for years.

Checkered Lilies are meadow flowers that will naturalize beautifully under the canopy of deciduous trees and shrubs. These adaptable bulbs thrive in either sun or partial shade.

Other Fritillaries are naturals in moist, woodsy settings. Try nestling them along a stone wall for a classic spring picture.

Crown Imperials in a naturaliz

The unusual Checkered Lily

PERFECT PARTNERS

The spring blooms of Fritillaries coincide with many other bulbs and early perennials, so it is easy to create colorful combinations.

Fritillaries in a woodland bed

ed bulb garden

Plant the clear yellow Crown Imperial 'Lutea' with soft pink Bleeding-hearts, vivid blue Jacob's Ladder, and a handful of lilac-purple Tulips for a colorful display of spring pastels.

In a bed of bulbs, combine the salmon Crown Imperial 'Aurora' and 'Apricot Beauty' Tulips. Accent these sunset colors with an edging of bright blue Grape Hyacinths.

Around a bench that is located under a favorite tree, scatter Checkered Lilies 'Purpurea', a purple-pink variety, and white 'Alba' with Glory-of-the-snow and Siberian Squills.

PLANTING & AFTERCARE

YOU WILL NEED: ❏ Fritillary bulbs ❏ Spade ❏ Trowel ❏ Compost ❏ Bone meal ❏ Mulch

1 **Plant bulbs** in early fall. Remove sod and loosen soil to a depth of 10 in., adding compost and bone meal to enrich planting area.

2 **Dig a 5 in. hole** for each bulb, spacing Crown Imperials 8-10 in. apart and other Fritillaries 2-6 in. apart, depending on bulb size.

3 **Place bulbs firmly** in holes, positioning them on their sides to help resist excess moisture. Cover with soil and water well.

4 **Cover area** with 2 in. of leaf mulch unless you are planting in grass. In grass, replace sod and firm it down well with your hands.

5 **If Crown Imperials** begin to lean, tie them to bamboo or metal stakes inserted firmly in the ground 4 in. away from the plant.

Tip

After three or four years your Crown Imperial bulbs should be dug up and divided. Replant bulblets as well as the parent bulb.

Secrets of Success

BUYING HINTS

● **Buy the largest** bulbs to get the biggest blooms. Feel each bulb to be sure that it is firm and plump.
● **Avoid bulbs** that are soft, moldy, or damaged. Do not buy Fritillary bulbs if their outer scales appear rubbed or damaged.

SUN & SOIL

● **Full sun or** partial shade. Fritillaries will bloom in a range of sunlight conditions, but full sun is best for the Crown Imperials.
● **Well-drained soil.** Fritillaries do well in moist, but not soggy, soil that is rich in organic matter.

SPECIAL ADVICE

● **Plant Fritillary bulbs** right away or store for a few days in moist peat moss to prevent them from drying.
● **Crown Imperials have** a musky odor that can be unpleasant. Avoid planting Crown Imperials close to a path, porch, or patio.

Seasonal Tips

EARLY FALL
Planting
Shop early to avoid bulbs that have been sitting on a hot, dry shelf. Plant bulbs as soon as possible. Mulch with a 1-2 in. layer of leaves or bark for protection.

EARLY SPRING
Fertilizing
Remove most of the winter mulch as the Fritillaries begin to emerge, leaving a thin layer to conserve moisture. Sprinkle bone meal around plants and scratch in lightly with a hand fork.

LATE SPRING
Cleaning up
Cut spent flowers from Fritillaries (below) so they will send their strength back into the bulbs for next year's blooms. Do not cut down foliage until it has withered and turned brown.

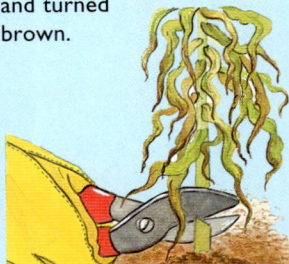

Plant Doctor

Leaf spot is a brown fungus that attacks Fritillary leaves and, in severe cases, flowers. Proper air circulation helps to prevent its growth and spread. In extreme cases of leaf spot, treat with a fungicide.

Glory-of-the-snow

Early flowers that sparkle like stars

Season	Special Features	Best Conditions	
✹ Flowers in early spring	✓ Easy to grow ❀ Disease resistant	🌐 Zones 4-7 ☀ Full sun or partial shade 🔧 Well-drained soil	Height: 5-10 in. ◄ Spread: 4-6 in.

Delicate Spring Sprites

Glory-of-the-snow brings a blanket of color to areas of lawn and tiny, tucked-away corners.

COLORS & VARIETIES

With their clusters of starry blossoms and grassy leaves, perky Glory-of-the-snow *(Chionodoxa)* embodies the optimism of spring. The blue, pink, or white blooms spread rapidly, but never seem out of place or unwelcome.

Blue, the pure blue of the reflected sky, is a common motivation for planting Glory-of-the-snow. For the largest and bluest blooms, choose 'Gigantea'.

'Pink Giant' was formerly rare, but it is becoming more widely available. It grows tall, to 10 in., and is a pretty, very pale shade of pink.

To duplicate the look of an old-fashioned garden, plant the sky blue, white-centered, 4-6 in. tall species *C. luciliae.* This species is a vigorous self-sower.

The flowers of *C. sardensis,* another old-fashioned species, are deep blue with a violet cast and

Vibrant C. sardensis

also have white centers. This species grows 4-8 in. tall.

WHERE TO PLANT

Wherever you plant Glory-of-the-snow bulbs, they will soon spread and find their own favorite spots, whether under a shrub, in the front of a flower bed, or in the lawn.

An area under shrubs is an ideal place for Glory-of-the-snow. It will get all the sun it needs before the shrubs' leaves emerge.

Tuck handfuls into a rock garden. While self-sown flowers will pop up here and there, the "polite" Glory-of-the-snow will never appear to crowd the other plants.

In a large planter, let Glory-of-the-snow create a carpet of color beneath a small tree or a hazy blue groundcover over which larger bulbs and other early blooming plants can hover.

The starry 'Pink Giant'

C. sardensis blankets the base o

PERFECT PARTNERS

Combine Glory-of-the-snow with other early bulbs for a sunny spring garden and pair it with groundcovers or woodland plants in sites with dappled or deep shade.

In a prominent flower bed, sky blue *C. luciliae*

In a lawn with Crocuses

f a tree in blue

'Blue Giant' is just the right height and color to interplant with yellow 'February Gold' Daffodils.

In a shady area, add bulbs of the pink *C. luciliae* 'Rosea' to a planting of Ferns and Hostas, which will just be emerging from the ground as the Glory-of-the-snow finish flowering.

Lily-of-the-valley is a good groundcover to accent with Glory-of-the-snow, as it is still small when the Glory-of-the-snow bloom. The hardy and vivid blue *C. forbesii* is vigorous enough to compete well.

Plant the white 'Alba' under a Forsythia for a fresh yellow-and-white spring duo. To spice up the effect, add early 'Red Emperor' Tulips to the sides of the planting.

PLANTING & AFTERCARE

YOU WILL NEED: ❏ Glory-of-the-snow bulbs ❏ Bulb planter ❏ Narrow trowel ❏ Bone meal

1 A bulb planter works best for naturalizing many bulbs. Push it 4 in. into the soil and pull out to remove a plug of soil.

2 Insert trowel in hole and loosen the soil at the bottom, mixing in a teaspoon of bone meal and a bit of compost or peat moss.

3 Set bulb, pointed end up, 3 in. deep in hole. Replace plug of soil and firm lightly. Vary spacing between bulbs for a natural look.

4 Rake area deeply to loosen surface soil and encourage self-sowing. Water planting area, unless rain is expected soon.

5 In spring when new shoots appear, sprinkle area with bone meal. Do not cut or deadhead dying flowers and foliage.

Troubleshooter

Glory-of-the-snow needs lots of moisture in spring. If rain is scarce, water regularly after it emerges until foliage dies.

Secrets of Success

BUYING HINTS

- **Buy large, firm bulbs.** Bulbs that measure an inch across, or larger, should each produce several flowering stems.
- **Avoid bulbs** that are soft or mushy. Do not buy those with scars, which could allow fungus to enter.

SUN & SOIL

- **Full sun to partial** shade. Summer shade is desirable, especially where summers are hot. At least half a day of spring sun will promote the best blooms.
- **Well-drained soil.** The soil should contain organic material to retain moisture.

SPECIAL ADVICE

- **After the first year,** the flower spikes will be smaller, but in a few years, new blooms will emerge.
- **Glory-of-the-snow** forces well for winter blooms indoors. Leave pots outdoors for ten weeks of cold before bringing in.

Seasonal Tips

FALL
Planting
Plant Glory-of-the-snow bulbs in early fall, as soon as they are available. Roots will grow in warm fall weather.

EARLY SPRING
Fertilizing
A light sprinkle of bone meal in early spring is all the fertilizer Glory-of-the-snow needs. Do not deadhead if you want it to spread.

EARLY SUMMER
Dividing
Glory-of-the-snow will usually increase without any help. If your stock is not growing as fast as you would like, lift the bulbs as they go dormant in early summer, separate the offsets (below), and replant immediately.

Plant Doctor

Bacterial diseases will often attack Glory-of-the-snow plants. Signs of disease include black or brown spots ringed in a second color. Rotate your plants annually to control the disease. If bacterial spot is a constant problem, try solarizing your soil.

Grape Hyacinths

Delicate spires of sapphire in spring

Season	Special Features	Best Conditions	
✹ **Blooms in spring**	✓ **Very easy care** ✂ **Good cut flower** 🕷 **Disease resistant**	🌐 **Zones 3-8** ☀ **Full sun to partial shade** 🔨 **Well-drained soil**	Height: 4-12 in. Spread: 3-8 in.

Vivid Elfin Blooms

Mass these brilliant flower bulbs with other spring bloomers for a showstopping display.

COLORS & VARIETIES

Grape Hyacinths *(Muscari)* are among the easiest bulbs to grow. In spring, they send up spikes of clustered flowers on short stems.

Blue is the typical color found among Grape Hyacinths, although some bicolored forms are available, such as *M. comosum*'s brownish yellow blooms tinged with purple.

For a unique look, pick *M. latifolium*, producing only a single broad leaf and a bicolored flower stalk with violet blooms on the bottom and deep blue flowers above.

For an unusual hue, try the sparkling white 'Album', which grows 5-10 in. tall. *M. armeniacum* 'Blue Spike' is a variety bearing stunning blue-purple blooms.

WHERE TO PLANT

Grape Hyacinths make a bold statement wherever you plant them. They are just as

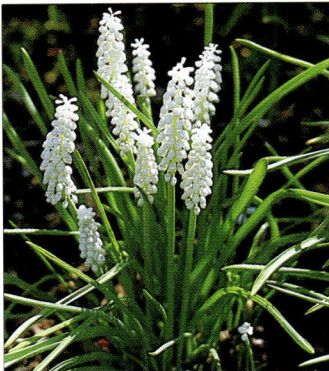
'Blue Spike' in a bulb garden

delightful in windowboxes and pots as they are in bulb borders and rock gardens.

Under a deciduous tree, Grape Hyacinths can get the sun they need before the tree grows leaves in late spring. These bulbs provide color in the garden before flowering trees bloom in spring.

Fill a rock garden with an assortment of small groups of Grape Hyacinths. Plant in masses, but allow enough space between them for their leaves to spread.

In a spring border, Grape Hyacinths offer radiant splashes of early color. Plant 'Plumosum', also known as Feather Hyacinth, for a very unusual look. Its plume of feathery, mauve flowers are carried on 8-12 in. stems.

In a large pot, the foliage of Grape Hyacinths gracefully fills out the container. Add other bulbs for a mix of interesting forms and shapes. Provide good drainage in the pot to prevent bulb rot.

The pure white 'Album'

Pink and yellow Daffodils, re...

PERFECT PARTNERS

Plant different varieties of Grape Hyacinths with other brightly colored, spring-blooming bulbs to march a parade of early spring color into your garden.

Pair brilliant blue Grape Hyacinths, such as the azure 'Muscari Blue', with vivid red Tulips. Plant these lower-growing Grape Hyacinths in front of the bright scarlet 'Red Riding Hood' Tulips for a brilliant display.

Create a spring meadow in a lawn with lavender and lilac Crocuses followed by lightly fragrant, cobalt blue 'Early Giant' and the black-blue, white-rimmed blooms of *M. neglectum*. Do not cut

Tulips, and M. latifolium

grass until the foliage of the bulbs has died back naturally.

Early spring-blooming shrubs and trees, such as Dogwoods and Azaleas, provide luscious color over the lavender-blue, deep blue-striped *M. azureum*.

A Grape Hyacinth partnership

PLANTING & AFTERCARE

YOU WILL NEED: ❑ Grape Hyacinth bulbs ❑ Bone meal ❑ Compost ❑ Trowel ❑ String ❑ Chicken wire

1 Prepare bed several weeks before planting the bulbs in early fall. Dig in compost and a cup of bone meal per square foot of bed.

2 Dig up bed at least 6-8 in. deep. Create the outline of the bed using string, making a curved drift for a more natural look.

3 Dig out the top 2-3 in. of soil. Set the bulbs in the soil, pointed ends up, spaced 4-5 in. apart. Cover bulbs with a layer of soil.

4 Lay chicken wire over bulbs to prevent rodents from eating. Sprinkle soil on top. Remove in spring before new growth emerges.

5 After the Hyacinths' foliage has died down in late spring or early summer, carefully rake it off. Remove and compost this material.

Dollar Sense

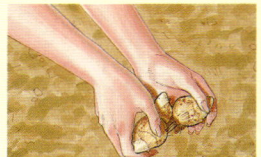

After a few years, lift and divide established Grape Hyacinth clumps after the foliage has died to increase their size.

Secrets of Success

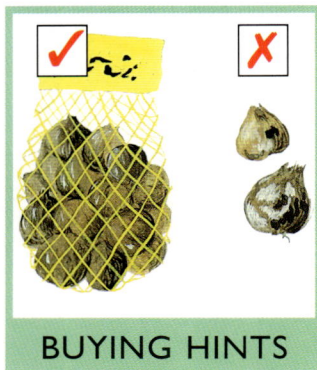

BUYING HINTS

SUN & SOIL

SPECIAL ADVICE

● **Buy large bulbs** that are firm to the touch in fall. Mail-order nurseries usually offer a greater selection than local nurseries.
● **Avoid bulbs** that are soft to the touch, as this is a sure sign of rot. Do not buy bulbs with spots or mildew.

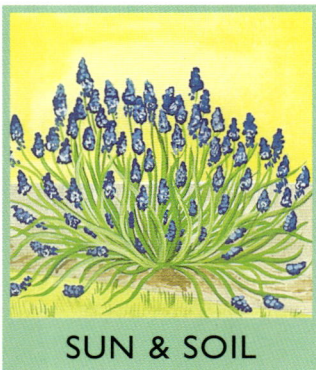

● **Full sun** to partial shade. In warmer areas of the country, plant Grape Hyacinths in partial shade to keep them blooming longer.
● **Rich, well-drained soil**. These bulbs like moist soil, but should be kept dry when not actively growing.

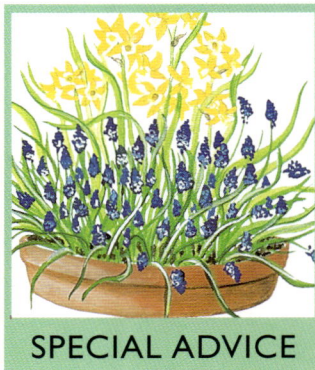

● **Do not fertilize** Grape Hyacinths, as they do not respond well to feeding after they are planted.
● **Grape Hyacinths** are terrific for forcing indoors. For a vibrant display, make a mixed bulb pot of Grape Hyacinths and Daffodils.

Seasonal Tips

EARLY FALL
Planting
Plant new Grape Hyacinth bulbs as soon as they are available in stores. Plant the bulbs you ordered from mail-order sources as soon as they arrive, after you have carefully ensured that they are in good condition. Store bulbs you intend to force for indoor displays in a refrigerator.

FALL
Forcing
Force the Grape Hyacinth bulbs you stored in early fall for indoor winter color.

EARLY SUMMER
Dividing
Grape Hyacinths naturalize and increase rapidly, forming large colonies that will bloom year after year. Divide bulbs, as you feel necessary, to increase your stock (below).

Plant Doctor

Rodents dig up and eat newly planted Grape Hyacinth bulbs. Plant your Grape Hyacinths with Daffodils or Scillas, both of which rodents dislike. You can also spray the soil with a mixture of pepper sauce and hot water.

Grecian Windflowers

Carpets of color to brighten spring days

Season	Special Features	Best Conditions	
✹ Flowers in mid-spring	✓ Easy to grow ❀ Disease resistant	🌐 Zones 4-8 ☀ Full sun or partial shade 🔱 Well-drained soil	Height: 3-8 in. Spread: 3-5 in.

Starry Spring Blooms

Grecian Windflowers spread rapidly into clouds of color in your flower bed or lawn.

COLORS & VARIETIES

Grecian Windflowers *(Anemone blanda)* produce Daisy-like flowers in pink, blue, or white for several weeks, and Fern-like foliage that disappears by early summer. Commonly sold as a mixture of all three hues, they are also available in single colors.

'White Splendour' has white petals and yellow centers, resembling a Daisy. It is the hardiest variety and the most vigorous spreader.

'Pink Star' is a widely available pink variety. Less common, but worth seeking out, is rose pink 'Charmer'.

'Blue Shades' is a variety whose color ranges from pale lilac to deep blue-purple, creating a shimmering blue sea in your garden.

WHERE TO PLANT

The soft hues and easy charm of Grecian Windflowers fit

The cool hues of 'Blue Star'

A naturalized planting

well almost anywhere in the landscape. These bulbs are not fussy about soil or site, as long as you avoid damp or deeply shaded spots.

Scatter handfuls of Grecian Windflowers in the lawn under deciduous trees. They compete well with grass and they will eventually spread into breathtaking carpets of color.

In a rock garden, these little bulbs find a happy home that duplicates their native environment. If they spread too quickly, it is easy to dig them up and move them to another site.

At the front edge of a flower bed, Grecian Windflowers will provide a pretty spring edging and then quickly disappear, making way for summer flowers.

Tuck small groups of Grecian Windflowers in bare spots along the edge of a path. They will quickly fill in and you will enjoy a close-up view of the spring blooms.

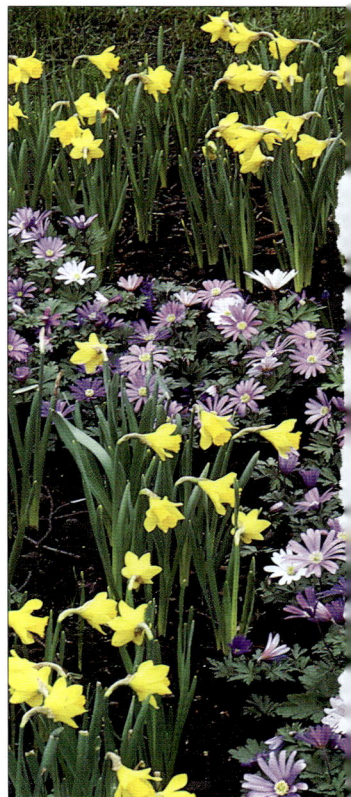

Blue and white Grecian Windflo[wers]

PERFECT PARTNERS

Grecian Windflowers make classic combinations with other mid-spring bulbs, flowering trees, and shrubs.

For a bold, color contrast, edge a planting of ivory white 'Mount Hood' Daffodils with white-centered, magenta 'Radar' Grecian Windflowers.

Naturalize 'Violet Star', or mixed colors of Grecian Windflowers, under a pale pink-flowering Crabapple tree. The low carpet of flowers will thrive in the tree's dappled shade.

Some herbs, such as Parsley and Basil, are slow starters in spring. Scatter pale pink 'Rosea' among

wers and Miniature Daffodils

them to bring early color to your herb garden.

Create a brilliant carpet of blue and gold spring flowers beneath a tree with deep blue 'Atrocaerulea' Grecian Windflowers, gold Crocuses, Grape Hyacinths, and sulphur yellow Daffodils.

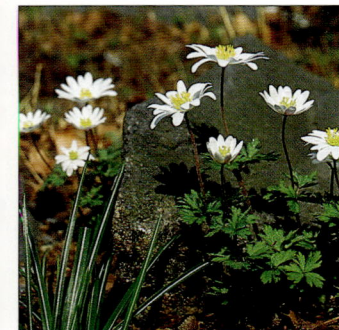

Cheery 'White Splendour'

PLANTING & AFTERCARE

YOU WILL NEED: ❏ Grecian Windflower tubers ❏ Garden fork ❏ Compost ❏ Bone meal

1 In early fall, plant Grecian Windflowers as soon as they are available. Soak tubers overnight in warm water before planting.

2 To naturalize Grecian Windflowers in grass, fork off sod. Add 1-2 in. of compost and sprinkle with bone meal. Dig in 6 in. deep.

3 Push tubers into the loosened soil sideways and 2 in. deep. Space them 3-4 in. apart and firm the soil lightly with your hands.

4 Replace the sod and water the entire area thoroughly to help the tubers start growing and the grass re-establish itself.

5 After flowers finish blooming, wait for leaves to disappear before mowing, or set mower high to leave the foliage intact.

Tip

If flowers decline after several years, dig up and divide tubers after foliage fades. Let dry for two days and then replant.

Secrets of Success

BUYING HINTS

- **Buy large, firm tubers** in early fall. Mail-order sources may offer a greater selection than nurseries.
- **Avoid late-fall** "bargain" tubers, as these will be planted too late to develop enough roots and ensure a good spring display.

SUN & SOIL

- **Full sun to partial** shade. Dappled shade from deciduous trees is ideal, but any exposure, except deep shade, will do.
- **Well-drained soil.** Avoid damp spots. Mulch Grecian Windflowers during long periods of drought.

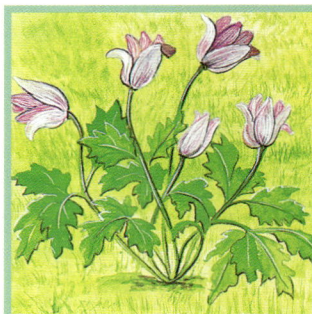

SPECIAL ADVICE

- **Windflowers often** close in cloudy weather. Do not worry; when the sun emerges, so will they.
- **Where summers are** hot, plant Grecian Windflowers where they will be shaded and kept cool by other plants.

Seasonal Tips

SUMMER
Ordering
Pre-order Windflowers now, as you may find the selection is limited at planting time.

EARLY FALL
Planting
Plant the tubers as soon as they are available. A long fall growing season will ensure the best blooms next spring. Divide established plantings.

SPRING
Maintaining
Fertilizing Grecian Windflowers is usually unnecessary, but a light dusting of bone meal, as the foliage emerges in early spring *(below)*, may improve performance in poor soil. Do not deadhead flowers, unless plants are spreading too vigorously. Leave foliage to strengthen the tubers.

Plant Doctor

Blister beetles may trouble Windflowers. These 3/4 in., shiny, black pests eat flower petals. Control them by shaking them loose and stepping on them or by spraying with rotenone. Discourage their return by placing pine or cedar branches around plants.

Large-cupped Daffodils

Sunny, ruffled blooms for sweeps of early color

Season	*Special Features*	*Best Conditions*	
✹ Flowers in spring	✓ Easy to grow ✂ Good for cutting ❫ Many varieties: fragrant	🌐 Zones 3-8 ☀ Full sun to partial shade 🔬 Well-drained soil	Height: 12-20 in. Spread: 6-8 in.

Bright Spring Sentinels

Large-cupped Daffodils offer large, cheerful blooms in a wide choice of colors.

COLORS & VARIETIES

Large-cupped Daffodils have ruffled cups that are shorter than their petals. Petals and cup are usually different shades, either yellow, white, orange, or pink, creating elegant combinations.

'Carlton' is the world's most popular Daffodil. The large, vanilla-scented blooms have clear yellow petals that contrast subtly, yet definitely, with the golden cups.

A great eyecatcher for planting with spring pastels, 'Ambergate' has coppery gold petals surrounding a red-orange cup. It holds its color best in partial shade.

The crisp, fragrant 'Ice Follies' looks cool when clear yellow cups open against white petals, but it serenely changes to warm cream over its long blooming season.

'Juanita' is one of the earliest Large-cups to flower. Orange-edged, golden cups give this yellow variety an

Naturalized in a lawn

unusual look that stands out in any planting.

WHERE TO PLANT

Big blooms on long stems ensure that Large-cupped Daffodils will make a splash wherever you plant them. They bring early color to beds and are easy to naturalize in grass or woods.

A small bed of Large-cupped Daffodils by the front door will brim with color over a long season. Plant a dozen each of several varieties for a cheerful show.

A row of dark, evergreen shrubs offers the opportunity to display these big, sunny blooms at their best. Plant in groups, using one variety for a formal look or several kinds for a cottage garden effect.

Large-cupped Daffodils make a stunning show in containers. Outdoors, they will bring early color to a porch or patio in spring. Or, use them to brighten an empty windowsill in winter.

'Salome' is lovely with bicolore

PERFECT PARTNERS

Combine Large-cupped Daffodils with early Tulips and spring-flowering shrubs and trees. Let their bold blooms accent the charms of daintier spring bulbs.

For an intricate composition of warm pastels, underplant a Dwarf Peach tree with apricot-edged, pure white 'Manon Lescaut' Daffodils. Underneath, add tiny, yellow-centered 'Lilac Wonder' Species Tulips.

The green-tinged, lemon blooms of 'St. Patrick's Day' appear at the same time as rich coral 'Toronto' Tulips and dusky blue Grape Hyacinths for a bold but not brash spring planting.

Fragrant 'Carlton' is a classic

d 'Ballade' Lily-flowered Tulips

Let the white petals and salmon-pink cups of large 'Coquille' brighten a planting of sweet-scented 'Delft Blue' Hyacinths while contributing a subtle scent of their own. A carpet of pale blue Creeping Phlox completes the picture.

Cool white 'Ben Hee'

PLANTING & AFTERCARE

YOU WILL NEED: ❑ Daffodil bulbs ❑ Stakes ❑ Trowel ❑ Bulb fertilizer ❑ Compost ❑ Mulch

1 **Plant Daffodils** in early fall. To plant along a path, push a stake into the ground to mark placement of each clump of bulbs.

2 **Evaluate** placement. An irregularly spaced arrangement looks more natural, while regular spacing looks very formal.

3 **At each stake,** dig an 8 in. deep, 1 ft. wide hole. Loosen the soil in the bottom of the hole, working in a handful of bulb fertilizer.

4 **Set nine to ten** bulbs in each hole, pointed ends up, spaced 3-4 in. apart. Push the base of each bulb gently into loose soil.

5 **Cover** with a mix of soil and compost. Firm soil with your hands and water well. Top with 2 in. of mulch to stop frost heaving.

Tip

Deadhead Daffodils to keep them from wasting energy producing seeds. Nourish with a sprinkling of bulb fertilizer each fall.

Secrets of Success

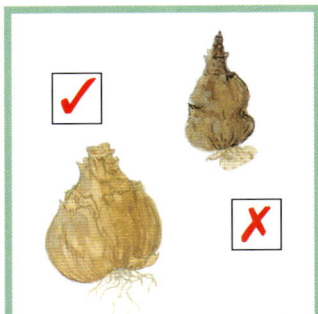

BUYING HINTS

- **Buy the largest bulbs** available. Large, double-nosed bulbs will produce at least two flowers each.
- **Avoid soft, bruised,** or moldy bulbs. Do not buy any that show cuts or scars, as they may carry diseases that can infect other bulbs.

SUN & SOIL

- **Full sun** to partial shade. Plants bloom best if they have full sun in spring, but they will not be harmed by partial shade in summer.
- **Well-drained soil.** Good drainage ensures a long life; in wet soils, add sand and compost or raise the beds.

SPECIAL ADVICE

- **To naturalize Daffodils** in woods, locate best spots to plant them by marking sunny areas in summer, when trees still have leaves.
- **Never cut or bundle** foliage; it must die back naturally to build strength for following years' blooms.

Seasonal Tips

EARLY FALL
Planting & Fertilizing
Plant new bulbs in outdoor containers *(below right)*, in the garden, and in pots to force for winter blooms indoors. Feed established plantings by sprinkling bulb fertilizer and scratching it into the soil over bulbs.

WINTER
Forcing
Keep potted bulbs in a cold spot for 14 weeks to grow roots, and then move to a cool, sunny window for early, indoor blooms.

SPRING—EARLY SUMMER
Cleaning up & Dividing
Remove faded flowers but leave foliage to grow. Wait until leaves have yellowed to remove and discard. Divide crowded bulbs and replant immediately, or store in a cool place to plant in fall.

Plant Doctor

Fire disease causes brown spots on the flowers of Large-cupped Daffodils. Prevent this fungal disease by removing and destroying Daffodil foliage after it dies back in late spring. Keeping the planting area clear of weeds will also reduce the incidence of fire disease.

Persian Ranunculus

Dazzling showstoppers to enliven garden designs

Season	Special Features	Best Conditions
✹ Flowers from spring to early summer	✂ Excellent cut flower	🌐 Zones 8-10
	✔ Easy care	☀ Full sun to partial shade
	🕷 Disease resistant	⛏ Well-drained, sandy soil

Height: 12-24 in.

◄ Spread: 5-8 in.

A Carnival of Color

The stunning blooms of Persian Ranunculus will provide riotous hues in sunny garden spots.

COLORS & VARIETIES

The petal-packed blooms of Persian Ranunculus *(R. asiaticus)* are borne on strong, 12-15 in. stems. Their vibrant blooms span the range of sunset hues, including gold, pink, rose, orange, yellow, red, and white. Their stunning colors and tall stems make Persian Ranunculus excellent cut flowers. The Fern-like foliage of these plants is handsome in the garden both before and after the flowers appear.

For blooms that look as delicate as tissue paper, but are vigorous enough to last for several weeks in the garden, try the ruffled petals of 'Tecolote Giants' in shades of solid red, gold, and orange, or picotee blooms that are edged with a second color. 'Color Carnival' offers gold, fuchsia, cream, neon orange, burgundy, or red blooms on 10 in. stems that are perfect for a windowbox, patio container, or clay pot.

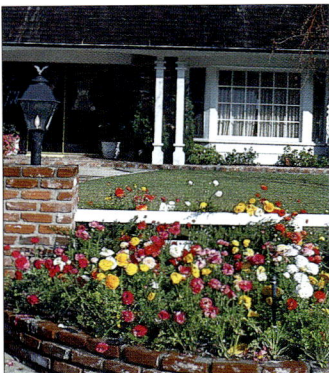

A brick bed of Ranunculus

'Double Persian Buttercup'

WHERE TO PLANT

Persian Ranunculus make a vivid accent wherever they are planted. They are very adaptable, fitting in well in containers or garden beds.

These complex, colorful blooms will be centerpieces in your cut-flower garden. They make long-lasting cut flowers, and their vivid hues add vibrancy to any bouquet.

In a rock garden, use Ranunculus individually or in groups of no more than five plants, so that they do not overwhelm the rest of the garden with their colors.

Add splashes of color to a flower border. Persian Ranunculus are scintillating accents whether used in the front, as an edging, or in the middle of the planting.

PERFECT PARTNERS

Match the exuberant hues of Persian Ranunculus with flowers in contrasting, cooler

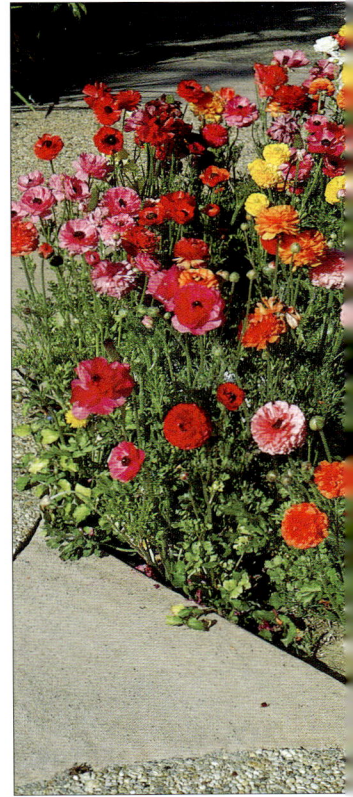

A sidewalk lined with the dusk

hues, or those with trailing habits that will set the stage for their erect form.

Combine the yellow 'Double Persian Buttercup' with white Candytuft and English Bluebells for a striking trio that is a knock-out in the late afternoon as the rays of the setting sun ignite their luminous shades. 'Double Persian Buttercup' is also available in red, orange, white, and pink hues.

Pair white Petunias or Geraniums with the Ranunculus 'Picotee' in a windowbox for blooms that will last from spring through summer. The bright, ruffled blooms of these Ranunculus are edged with a second color and will electrify the

hues of Ranunculus

elegant, ivory hues of the trailing plants.

Display the multicolored hues of the 8-10 in. tall 'Bloomingdale' in a large pot with white Sweet Alyssum blooms, surrounded by decorative sphagnum moss.

Deep red 'Tecolote Giants'

PLANTING & AFTERCARE

YOU WILL NEED: ❏ Persian Ranunculus bulbs ❏ Compost ❏ Ground limestone ❏ Cottonseed meal

1 Prepare the bed well before you plant the Ranunculus. Spread a 4 in. layer of well-rotted manure or compost on soil.

2 Dig I cup of ground limestone per square foot into bed to 6-8 in. Soak bulbs in tepid water or weak vitamin solution overnight.

3 Poke a 2 in. deep hole in soil with index finger. Place bulb in hole with "claws" facing down. Allow 6 in. between bulbs.

4 When plants are 2-3 in. tall, make a I in. by I in. trench between them. Add cottonseed meal to trench at a rate of I tsp. per plant.

5 Water well. When buds appear, feed with a liquid fertilizer. Deadhead faded blooms regularly to keep the plants looking neat.

Tip

For the best growth and best blooms, dig up bulbs after foliage dies and store indoors in a cool, dry place. Replant the following year.

Secrets of Success

BUYING HINTS

● **Buy large, firm bulbs** in fall that have four or more sturdy "claws". Look to mail-order catalogs for individual colors.
● **Avoid bulbs** that are soft to the touch, as they have been exposed to moisture and will most likely rot.

SUN & SOIL

● **Full sun.** In extremely hot climates, plant the bulbs in a shadier location to protect the plants from midday heat.
● **Rich, well-drained soil.** Persian Ranunculus prefer dry soil around their stems and moist soil around their roots. Ensure good drainage.

SPECIAL ADVICE

● **If you plant** Ranunculus in early fall in areas with no winter frost, the plants will bloom earlier than those planted in late winter.
● **In cold climates,** grow Ranunculus in flats indoors on a windowsill. Transplant into garden after frosts.

Seasonal Tips

FALL
Planting
In zones 8-10, plant Persian Ranunculus bulbs outdoors in fall. Apply a light mulch where unseasonal frosts might occur.

LATE WINTER
Planting
In colder climates, plant your Persian Ranunculus inside in containers (*right*) for an early show of indoor color.

SPRING
Planting
In zones 4-7, start Ranunculus bulbs outdoors after all danger of frost has passed. In the coldest climates, start bulbs in trays of well-drained potting soil for planting outdoors after the danger of frost has passed. Keep the soil moist, but not soggy.

Plant Doctor

Root rot causes the plant's claw-like roots to rot, killing the plant. This will occur if plants are overwatered prior to root formation. Water well after planting and not again until plants sprout. Resume regular watering after they sprout.

Poppy Anemones

Silky petals to sway in summer breezes

Season	Special Features	Best Conditions
✳ Flowers in late spring or early summer	✓ **Easy to grow**	🌐 **All zones**
	✳ **Disease resistant**	☀ **Full sun or partial shade**
	✂ **Good for cut flowers**	🌱 **Well-drained soil**

Height: 10-18 in.

Spread: 3-4 in.

Spritely Dancing Blooms

Poppy Anemones bring vivid color, graceful movement, and long-lasting charm to gardens.

COLORS & VARIETIES

Poppy Anemones *(Anemone coronaria)* flower in vibrant shades of red, blue, pink, and white. They resemble Poppies with their black centers and strong stems, but their cup-shaped blooms last much longer.

The '**De Caen Series'** offers open flowers in scarlet, pink, purple, or white with a single row of petals. Framed by deeply lobed, frilly leaves, 'Sylphide' is a soft rose-lilac, while 'Hollandia' offers a bold splash of scarlet.

'**St. Brigid' Anemones** are more ornate double-flowering types. The 'Mt. Everest' variety is a classic white, as snowy as its name.

WHERE TO PLANT

All Poppy Anemones have a wildflower grace that suits a

The radiant red 'Hollandia'

wide variety of settings—from the most natural to the most formal.

The intense colors of Poppy Anemones add gaiety to spring and summer flower beds. Tuck groups of five to ten tubers into any empty nook. For portable color, plant bulbs in pots.

Grow a row of Poppy Anemones in your vegetable garden to cut for summer bouquets. Plant a handful every week throughout spring for continuous bloom.

In zones 8-10, where Poppy Anemones can be left in the ground year-round, they will make happy additions to rock gardens, where these spritely flowers look perfectly at home.

PERFECT PARTNERS

Versatile Poppy Anemones are ideal mates for many

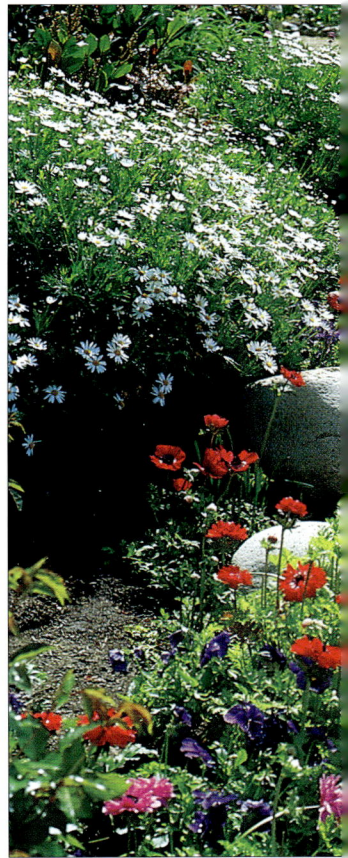

'St. Brigid' Anemones in a sum

early summer perennials and bulbs. They also provide striking punctuation to beds of annual plants.

Edge a planting of Asiatic Lilies with 'Mr. Fokker' Anemones. The Fern-like Anemone foliage and the dark blue blooms are a delightful complement to the warm-toned Lilies.

Combine the pure white Anemone 'The Bride' with silver Dusty Miller and white Verbena for an easy-care planting that will look fresh and clean all summer long.

Poppy Anemones offer an airy contrast to spiky Gladiolus blooms. Plant the bright blue 'Lord Lieutenant'

Naturalized Anemones

...er border

with cool pink, rose, and violet Gladioli for a romantic early summer border.

Tip

All Poppy Anemone bulbs require well-drained soil. To determine if your planting site has adequate drainage, dig a hole at the depth bulbs will be planted. Fill the hole with water and let soak in. Repeat two more times, the last time noting how long it takes for the water to be absorbed. If it takes six hours or more, drainage is not adequate and you should look for another site.

PLANTING & AFTERCARE

YOU WILL NEED: ❑ Poppy Anemone tubers ❑ Trowel ❑ Compost ❑ Bone meal ❑ Lime ❑ Mulch

1 **Soak tubers** overnight in warm water before planting. Plant Poppy Anemones in fall in zones 8-10, in spring in zones 5-7.

2 **Dig your garden** or lawn planting area to a depth of 6 in. and mix in a small handful of bone meal and lime if your soil is acidic.

3 **Push the tubers** sideways 2 in. into the loosened soil. Space 3-4 in. apart. Firm the soil lightly with your hands.

4 **Water well.** Replace sod (if planting in lawn). Cover with 1-2 in. of mulch to retain moisture and insulate tubers.

5 **In areas colder** than zone 8, lift Poppy Anemones before fall frost. Store tubers over winter in a dry, frost-free place.

Tip

Plant tubers in groups for the best effect. Plant five to ten Poppy Anemones together for a cheery display.

Secrets of Success

BUYING HINTS

- **Buy large, firm tubers** in early fall. Mail-order sources will often have a greater selection of Poppy Anemones than nurseries.
- **Avoid small tubers** or those with spots or any blemishes that may indicate disease or bruising.

SUN & SOIL

- **Full sun or partial** shade. In hotter zones, provide some shade. In cooler zones, provide plants with full sun.
- **Well-drained soil.** Avoid planting where moisture collects. Add compost and sand to loosen clay soils.

SPECIAL ADVICE

- **Avoid tubers** collected in the wild; several varieties are endangered. Look for a label stating tubers were nursery-propagated.
- **In hot areas,** plant Poppy Anemones in crevices between rocks where roots remain cooler.

Seasonal Tips

EARLY FALL
Digging & Storing
In zones 2-7, lift, dry, and store Poppy Anemones. Keep the tubers in a dry, frost-free place over winter. Make sure your storage area provides proper air circulation to prevent moisture from collecting and tubers from rotting.

FALL
Warm-climate Planting
In zones 8-10, be sure to plant Poppy Anemones before the first frost for mid- to late-spring blooms.

EARLY TO LATE SPRING
Planting
Plant Poppy Anemones for mid- to late-summer blooms. Plant a new batch each week for constant color. Add to vegetable beds and borders to brighten before the vegetables ripen *(below)*.

Plant Doctor

Poor air circulation among the foliage of closely planted bulbs may invite diseases including powdery mildew, evidenced by a whitish dust on leaves, and leaf spot, which causes brown spots on leaves. Both can be controlled with fungicide applications.

Scillas

Sheets of bloom to color shady spots

Season	Special Features	Best Conditions	
✹ Flowers in spring	✓ Easy to grow	🌐 Zones 2-10	
	✢ Self-seeds freely	☀ Partial to full shade	Height: 4-15 in.
	✳ Disease and pest resistant	⬎ Well-drained soil	← Spread: 3-8 in.

Beautiful Pastel Bells

Scillas bloom in waves of beautiful color, brightening up shady corners of every garden.

COLORS & VARIETIES

Although traditionally blue, Scillas also bloom in shades of pink, lavender, or white. The dainty, bell-shaped blooms perch above strap-like leaves. Quite happy in shade, Scillas rapidly spread to create a wash of color. A variety exists for virtually every growing climate.

Siberian Squills (*Scilla siberica*), hardy in zones 2-8, are the most familiar Scillas, with nodding, intense blue bells on 4-6 in. stems. A lovely, pure white form, 'Alba', is also available.

Spanish Bluebells (*S. campanulata*) form large clusters of blue, pink, or white flowers on 10-15 in. stems in zones 3-9. Try 'Dainty Maid' for lovely mauve-pink blooms.

Peruvian Squill or Cuban Lily (*S. peruviana*) is the best Scilla for zones 8-10. The starry, rich violet-blue flower clusters are held on 8-10 in. stems.

Spires of Chinese Squill

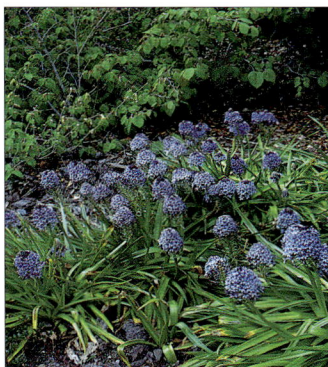

Starry Peruvian Squill blooms

WHERE TO PLANT

Vigorous, spreading Scillas produce bold strokes of color in spring gardens. Plant them where they can spread freely and make the most of their willingness to bloom in partial to full shade.

Siberian Squills are lovely scattered in the lawn or colonizing the ground beneath shrubs. They also embellish the rock garden with patches of dainty, blue bells in early spring.

Spanish Bluebells are a breathtaking sight in the woodlands, spreading into a flowery carpet. Try them in shady beds as well, where deadheading will easily curb their wandering ways.

Peruvian Squills grow well in poor, stony soil, which makes them ideal for planting on difficult slopes. However, do not limit their use as they will contribute a great deal to the beauty of any partially shaded shrub garden or flower bed.

The rich indigo blooms of Sibe

PERFECT PARTNERS

The soft pastel blooms of all Scillas blend well with many other bulbs, flowering shrubs, and trees, creating layers of gentle color in the spring garden.

Herald the new season with blue and gold. Plant royal blue Siberian Squills 'Spring Beauty' under a Forsythia and add clumps of yellow 'Jetfire' Narcissi.

Underplant pink-flowering Magnolias with drifts of pale violet 'Excelsior' Spanish Bluebells to produce a romantic scene.

Echo the overhead blooms of a pink-flowering Crabapple tree with a planting of rosy pink

ian Squill

'Rosabella' Spanish Bluebells. Complete the picture with a scattering of dainty, pale blue Forget-me-nots.

Spanish Bluebells and Azaleas

PLANTING & AFTERCARE

YOU WILL NEED: ❑ Scilla bulbs ❑ Small stakes ❑ Garden gloves ❑ Trowel ❑ Bone meal

1 **To naturalize Scillas** in a woodland, stake a spot for each bulb. Arrange in a natural-looking group, spacing irregularly 3-12 in. apart.

2 **Wearing gloves** to prevent blisters, thrust the trowel vertically a full-blade depth into the soil. Wiggle to loosen the soil.

3 **Add 1 tsp.** of bone meal to each blade slit and insert bulb, pointed end up, to a depth of 4 in. Firm soil around each bulb.

4 **Mark the perimeters** of the area with stakes to prevent inadvertently trampling the bulbs. Water well. Fallen leaves will mulch.

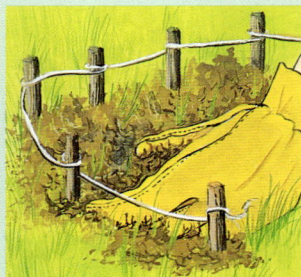

5 **In late spring,** top planting area with a layer of compost to gently fertilize and help Scillas spread naturally.

Tip

In natural plantings, Scillas spread over time if they remain undisturbed. There is no need to deadhead them.

Secrets of Success

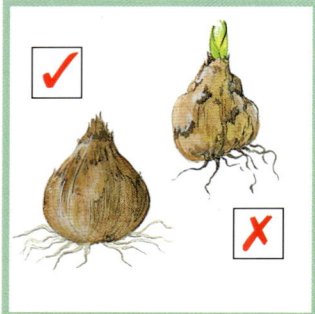

BUYING HINTS

- **Buy large, plump** Scilla bulbs that feel firm and smooth, as soon as they are available in the fall.
- **Avoid bulbs that are** soft, moldy, or appear bruised. Do not buy bulbs that have sprouted any new growth at their tips.

SUN & SOIL

- **Partial to full shade.** Scillas are one of the few bulbs that will readily bloom in dense shade, such as that under evergreens.
- **Well-drained soil.** Scillas will grow in poor, dry soil, but will bloom and spread better in rich, moist soil.

SPECIAL ADVICE

- **Prevent the rapid** spread of Scillas in flower beds by removing flowers before seeds have had a chance to form and drop.
- **Interplant Scillas** among bulbs that mice regularly devour. The mild Onion smell of Scilla repels them.

Seasonal Tips

EARLY FALL
Planting
Plant Scilla bulbs as soon as they are available from nurseries or mail-order sources. Early planting allows plenty of time for strong root growth before the ground freezes.

LATE SPRING
Cleaning up & Dividing
Cut back the Scilla foliage after it dies. Add 1-2 in. of compost over planting site to conserve moisture and enrich the soil. After several years, when Scilla clumps are thick, you can dig them up to start new plantings in other areas. After foliage has withered, dig up and carefully separate Scilla bulbs (below). Replant following the directions for new bulbs.

Plant Doctor

Scilla bulbs can be attacked by bulb mites. The tiny, whitish yellow pests, often with two brown spots, are found on decaying foliage and rotting bulbs. Mites burrow into bulbs, spreading disease. Control by discarding all rotting or wounded bulbs.

Single Early Tulips

A blaze of color to greet spring

Season

* Flowers in early spring

Special Features

* ✓ Easy to grow
* ✂ Good for cutting
* Disease resistant

Best Conditions

* 🌐 Zones 3-8
* ☀ Full sun to partial shade
* Well-drained soil

Height: 10-16 in.

Spread: 6-12 in.

Brilliant Cups of Color

It would hardly seem like spring without the classic blooms of Single Early Tulips.

COLORS & VARIETIES

Single Early means early-blooming Tulips that have one flower to a stem and six petals to a flower. This class of Tulips includes many of the old favorites that greet spring in every front yard, and exciting new varieties.

Wildly popular in recent years, hybrid 'Apricot Beauty' offers blended shades of salmon and pastel pink.

Look to orange Single Early Tulips for fragrance. 'Princess Irene' has subtle brushstrokes of violet on sunset-hued petals, and 'General de Wet' is a translucent golden orange. Both have a sweet scent.

If spring is incomplete without red Tulips, try 'Coleur Cardinal', which is a striking red. For a classic clear yellow, choose fragrant 'Bellona' for a fresh look. In some settings, an elegant white Single Early Tulip is the best choice. 'Diana' is

'General de Wet' by stone wall

flawless and pairs well with violet 'Van der Neer'.

WHERE TO PLANT

Single Early Tulips are just about foolproof. Blooming at a time when color is welcome everywhere, they are modestly sized to fit easily in any space. Properly planted, they will flower well for several years.

Plant Single Early Tulips in your most visible spots. A clump or two of bulbs by the mailbox, in front of a foundation planting of evergreen shrubs, or at the foot of the drive will offer a cheerful view to passersby.

Let these inexpensive bulbs bring your perennial bed to life weeks before most other plants show much color. A few groups of 10 or 12 bulbs will inaugurate the gardening season.

In a windowbox or an outdoor planter, these Tulips make a cheerful show. Many varieties also force easily

Vibrant 'Coleur Cardinal'

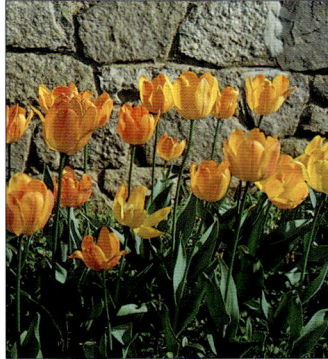

Sweetly scented 'Bellona' with r

indoors to anticipate spring in a most colorful way.

PERFECT PARTNERS

Single Early Tulips are bold enough to make beautiful partnerships with spring-flowering shrubs and trees. They also combine well with other spring bulbs and early-blooming perennials.

Underscore the rosy pink spring blooms of a Peach tree with an echo of the satin-petalled, cherry pink 'Christmas Marvel'. Include 'White Splendour' Grecian Windflowers for a complete picture. Or, below a coral Flowering Quince plant ruffled, peachy pink 'Beauty Queen' Tulips, a variety that grows to 18 in. tall.

Punctuate a drift of mid-season Daffodils, such as

ddish orange Crown Imperials

lemon 'Daydream', with the red-and-yellow 'Grand Duc' ('Keiserskroon') Single Early Tulips. Both of these bulbs offer a light, sweet fragrance.

A clear yellow Single Early Tulip, such as lovely 'Yokohama', in a bed of soft blue Pansies 'Blues Jam' with a fluffy edging of snow white Candytufts paints a fresh garden picture in spring.

Popular 'Apricot Beauty'

PLANTING & AFTERCARE

YOU WILL NEED: ❑ 12 Single Early Tulip bulbs
❑ Spade ❑ Sand ❑ Bulb fertilizer ❑ Lime ❑ Mulch

1 Plant Tulips in fall. To plant in fresh soil, such as near a road, dig out the soil 14 in. deep, making the hole 1 ft. across for 12 bulbs.

2 Put a 2 in. layer of sand in bottom of the hole. Add 2 in. of soil, bulb fertilizer, and, if soil is acidic, some lime. Mix and level soil.

3 Add a 2 in. layer of plain soil, level, and set in bulbs 3 in. apart, pointed ends up. Cover bulbs with remaining soil.

4 Firm soil with hands and water well. Add a 2 in. layer of mulch. Mark the planting area to avoid trampling shoots in spring.

5 Remove mulch in early spring when Tulips emerge. In fall, sprinkle bulb fertilizer around bulbs and replace mulch.

Tip

When Single Early Tulips stop blooming well after a few years, dig up bulbs and replace with new Single Early Tulips.

Secrets of Success

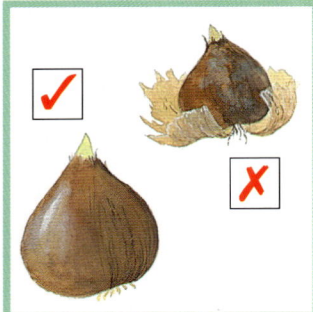

BUYING HINTS

SUN & SOIL

SPECIAL ADVICE

● **Buy Tulip bulbs** in early fall as soon as they are available. Look for big, firm, plump bulbs with tight-fitting, shiny, brown skins.
● **Avoid very small** Tulip bulbs. Do not buy any that are moldy or have already begun to sprout.

● **Full sun** to partial shade. Single Early Tulips do best with full sun, but tolerate some light afternoon shade.
● **Well-drained soil.** Excess moisture in the soil, especially during summer, will rot bulbs, but do not let bulbs dry out in spring.

● **Single Early Tulips** grow well and often rebloom better in very well-drained, gravel-like soil.
● **In zones 8-10,** chill Tulip bulbs for three months in refrigerator before planting in early winter. They will bloom beautifully in spring.

Seasonal Tips

FALL
Planting
Where winters are cold, plant Tulips a month after first hard frost. Waiting until soil has cooled ensures good root growth and prevents fall sprouting. Fertilize established plantings with a balanced bulb fertilizer.

SPRING
Deadheading & Lifting
Cut off faded flowers to strengthen the bulbs. Wait until foliage has withered to remove it *(right)* and add to your compost pile.

SUMMER
Digging up
Avoid summer watering of areas planted with Tulips. In damp climates, dig up the bulbs after their foliage has completely withered. Store in a cool, dark place and replant outside in fall.

Plant Doctor

Tulip break is a virus that causes contrasting color streaks on the flower petals. While some people like the appearance, the infected Tulips will slowly decline. Move uninfected bulbs to a new spot, and avoid replanting Tulips in the area for several years.

Striped Squills

Stalks of ice blue bells for the spring garden

Season	Special Features	Best Conditions	
✹ Flowers in early spring	✓ Easy to grow ⚬ Fragrant ✱ Disease resistant	🌐 Zones 3-9 ☀ Full sun to partial shade 🔧 Moist, well-drained soil	Height: 4-8 in. ← Spread: 2-4 in.

Frilly Spikes of Blooms

The pale blue bells of Striped Squills return each year to embellish early spring gardens.

COLORS & VARIETIES

Striped Squills are close relatives of Siberian Squills, but they belong to the genus *Puschkinia*. They show their family resemblance by producing dense clusters of bell-shaped, lightly fragrant, blue or white blooms on 6 in. stems in early spring.

Usually there are only two grass-like leaves, which elongate to 8-10 in. as the flowers fade. These die back in late spring and disappear.

The form of Striped Squill that is commonly available looks pale blue in the garden, but when examined closely it reveals bluish white petals, each with a central stripe of bright blue.

The selection 'Alba' is pure white and gives a bright effect that looks especially showy from a distance. It tends to bloom even earlier than the common form. As 'Alba' is somewhat rare, it can be hard to find.

Striped Puschkinia scilloides

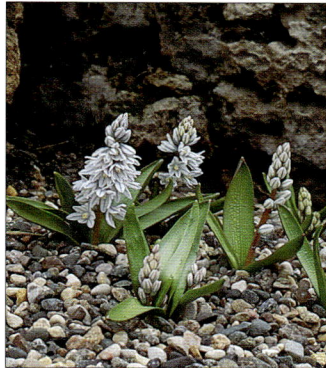

Spring color in a rock garden

WHERE TO PLANT

Striped Squills deserve a place in any spring garden, where they will return each year, slowly spreading into large clumps. They will also appear in new places in the garden from self-seeding.

Striped Squills show off their charms beautifully in a rock garden. They never become invasive, and their cool blue color tempers the bright shades of many other spring alpines.

Let Striped Squills provide a lacy edging along a path, perhaps in front of other early bulbs. They will not flop onto the path and will disappear quietly when their early flowering season comes to an end.

Plant them in masses under a tree or shrub to provide a seasonal flowering groundcover. Or, scatter them in generous groups in flower beds; Striped Squills always attract attention in the spring landscape.

Striped Squills bloom at the sa

PERFECT PARTNERS

The pale hues and dainty form of Striped Squills go well with everything. Be sure to plant them in the front row of any combination so they will not be hidden by taller plants.

In the grass under early-blooming ornamental trees, Striped Squills produce a haze of color. The soft blue of the common form sets off the rich pink of a 'Peggy Clarke' Japanese Apricot.

Combine clear pink Creeping Phlox 'Millstream Daphne', white 'Carpet of Snow' Sweet Alyssums, and pale blue Striped Squills to carpet a rock garden with spring pastels.

ne time as early Daffodils

Embellish a planting of small 'Violet Pearl' Species Tulips and early 'February Gold' Daffodils with a dainty highlight of white 'Alba' Striped Squills.

Early blooming, white 'Alba'

PLANTING & AFTERCARE

YOU WILL NEED: ❏ 100 Striped Squill bulbs ❏ Trowel ❏ Compost or leaf mold ❏ Mulch

1 **Plant Striped Squills** in early fall. To plant a 6 in. wide edging, allow 12 bulbs per running foot. Dig out soil to a depth of 6 in.

2 **Replace a 2 in. layer** of equal parts soil and compost in trench bottom. Level mix and firm it lightly, but do not compact it.

3 **Set bulbs** 2 in. apart in double rows, pointed ends up. Gently replace soil, carefully mixing in more compost if the soil is poor.

4 **Firm soil** with palms of your hands and water thoroughly. Top with 1 in. of loose mulch to prevent frost heaving over winter.

5 **Remove** spent blooms, unless you want them to self-sow, but let foliage die back naturally. Plants do not need fertilizing or dividing.

Tip

Unlike many bulbs, Striped Squills do not like to be baked dry during their summer dormancy. Water during dry spells.

Secrets of Success

BUYING HINTS

● **Buy firm bulbs** with pale tan, papery skins. Look for the largest bulbs, which are only ½ in. in diameter.
● **Avoid soft, moldy,** or dried-out bulbs. Tiny, ivory shoots may show at bulb tips, but do not buy any bulbs with long shoots.

SUN & SOIL

● **Full sun** to partial shade. Striped Squills need sun in spring, but partial shade in summer will help to keep the soil moist.
● **Well-drained soil.** These bulbs are not fussy about soil, as long as it drains well and stays moist year-round.

SPECIAL ADVICE

● **Striped Squills** may bloom at ground level their first spring. After they have acclimated a year, they will bloom at normal height.
● **Striped Squills** do not like to be disturbed. For the best showing year after year, do not divide.

Seasonal Tips

EARLY FALL
Planting
Plant Striped Squills as soon as they are available. If left unplanted for long, they become dry and lose vigor. Pot up six bulbs in a 6 in. pot for indoor forcing.

LATE WINTER
Forcing
Striped Squills need at least 14 weeks of cool storage to grow roots, so wait until late winter to bring your pots indoors for forcing (right). After forcing, move the pots outside.

SPRING
Cleaning up
Deadhead spent blooms, unless you want the bulbs to self-sow. Plant forced bulbs as soon as soil is workable, disturbing the roots as little as possible. Wait until foliage dies before cutting it back.

Plant Doctor

Striped Squills are usually free of any diseases or pests, but in rare cases may be troubled by aphids. These yellowish green insects feed on leaf and stem juices, weakening the plant. To control, cut off and destroy infected parts, or use insecticidal soap.

Triumph Tulips

Mid-spring beauties offer a bounty of color

Season

✿ Flowers in mid-spring

Special Features

✓ Easy to grow

🌿 Wind resistant

✂ Good for cutting

✗ Edible flowers

Best Conditions

🌐 Zones 3-8

☀ Full sun or partial shade

⛏ Well-drained soil

Height: 12-18 in.

Spread: 8-10 in.

Spring's Rainbow

Versatile Triumph Tulips combine classic beauty with exceptional, easy-care features.

COLORS & VARIETIES

Triumphs are medium-sized, mid-season Tulips whose strong stems weather wind and rain. After blooming, the foliage dies back quickly to make way for other summer flowers. Triumphs come in all colors except blue, and offer a range of bicolors.

The Triumph class includes varieties that last more years than many Tulips. Both lavender-pink 'Don Quichotte' and yellow-edged, red 'Kees Nelis' enjoy excellent comeback records.

These cool-season bulbs need to "winter" in a refrigerator to bloom in the deep South. Pink-and-white 'Blenda', buttercup yellow 'Golden Melody', and pure white 'Hibernia' are top choices for Southern gardens and indoor forcing.

'**New Design**' is exciting for its unusual, white-edged foliage, as well as its cream blooms brushed with pink.

'Bastogne' and Pansies

Pink-and-white 'Garden Party'

WHERE TO PLANT

Triumphs belong anywhere you want a dash of spring color. At home in formal beds, informal plantings, and containers, they virtually guarantee success in any planting situation.

Formal beds call for symmetrical perfection, which is easy to achieve with Triumph Tulips. Choose one or two varieties and plant them in a mass to create an elegant sweep of bloom.

Handle Triumphs informally for cheerful splashes of color. Plant them in groups of a dozen bulbs in a perennial border or among shrubs in a bed.

Triumphs shine in windowboxes or containers where they will decorate any home with a crayon-box vision of spring. When they stop blooming, bulbs can be lifted or left in place and overplanted with annuals to hide fading foliage.

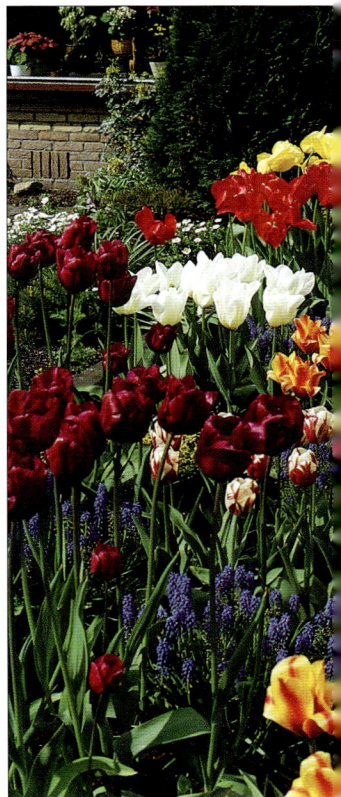

Triumph Tulips and Grape Hy

PERFECT PARTNERS

Triumph Tulips are available in so many colors that you can create any color scheme you have in mind, whether you use the Triumphs alone or combine them with other flowers.

The gorgeous, buttery shade of 'Yellow Present' blends well with pastels. Plant it behind blue Jacob's Ladder in the perennial bed, or grow it in a tub with an edging of pink Pansies.

In front of an evergreen hedge, place a group of glowing 'Orange Wonder' next to an equal-sized clump of icy white 'Snowstar' to create a showstopping fire-and-ice display.

...cinths light up a spring garden

Bring cool purple hues to your garden by planting violet-blue Forget-me-nots and lavender-and-white 'Dreaming Maid' Triumphs under a Lilac bush.

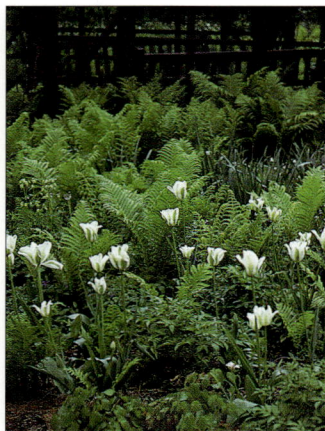

'Angel' with Cinnamon Ferns

PLANTING & AFTERCARE

YOU WILL NEED: ❏ Triumph Tulip bulbs ❏ Mulch ❏ Shovel ❏ Bone meal ❏ Rake ❏ Yardstick

1 **For a formal bed,** prepare planting area in fall. Remove soil to a depth of 8 in. and set aside. Sprinkle bed with bone meal.

2 **Loosen soil** in bottom of bed an additional 8 in., mixing in the bone meal. Add sand to improve drainage in heavy soil.

3 **Rake bottom** of bed to a smooth, level surface. Bulbs must all be planted at the same depth to ensure simultaneous blooms.

4 **Use a yardstick** to space the bulbs exactly 4 in. apart in each direction, placing them firmly, pointed ends up, all at the same level.

5 **Replace soil,** taking care not to disturb bulbs. Water well. Add 2 in. of mulch. Sprinkle with bone meal in spring.

Tip

Do not cut Tulip leaves or dig bulbs until leaves have faded. Bulbs use fading leaves as "food". Cutting too early may reduce future blooming.

Secrets of Success

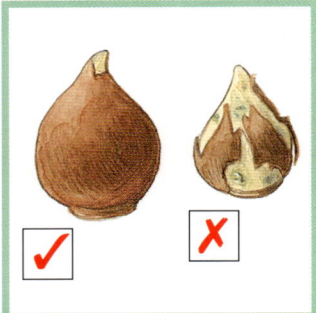

BUYING HINTS

- **Buy Tulip bulbs** in fall. Choose firm, plump bulbs in the largest size available for the largest blooms.
- **Avoid soft, moldy** bulbs and those that have begun to sprout. Do not buy those with loose or damaged papery coverings.

SUN & SOIL

- **Full sun to partial** shade. Half a day of sun is sufficient in climates where hot spring temperatures can shorten bloom time.
- **Well-drained soil.** Excess moisture will cause bulbs to break into little non-blooming bulblets.

SPECIAL ADVICE

- **For more years** of blooms, improve soil drainage before planting and set bulbs several inches deeper than recommended.
- **When planting Tulips** in a container, position bulbs with flat sides facing out so leaves drape over the edge.

Seasonal Tips

FALL
Planting
Plant Triumph Tulips three or four weeks after the first killing frost. Pot some up for indoors. In zones 9-10, or for indoor forcing, mimic winter by chilling bulbs in the refrigerator for ten weeks before planting.

WINTER
Planting & Forcing
In warm climates, plant chilled bulbs in the garden. Bring potted bulbs into room temperature to force early blooms.

SPRING
Deadheading & Lifting
Cut off faded flowers to strengthen the bulbs (below). Dig up bulbs from containers and formal beds when foliage has withered and store in a dry place for fall planting. Leave other bulbs in ground.

Plant Doctor

Deer will eat Tulips to the ground. The best solution is to plant your Tulips in a fenced area, or in containers close to the house, where they can be protected. The smell from a sprinkling of bone meal or blood meal will also help to discourage deer.

White Daffodils

Serene blooms that gleam in the spring garden

Season	Special Features	Best Conditions	
✹ Flowers in spring	✓ Easy to grow ✂ Good for cutting ⚘ Many varieties: fragrant	🌐 Zones 3-8 ☀ Full sun to partial shade 🛠 Well-drained soil	Height: 6-20 in. Spread: 4-8 in.

Enchantment in Spring

White Daffodils come in many sizes and shapes, adding grace and elegance to any garden.

COLORS & VARIETIES

White Daffodils offer a pleasing variety of flower shapes. Cups range from large to small and may be ruffled or split. The petals may be swept-back, ruffled, or double. Many varieties possess a sweet fragrance.

All-time classic 'Mount Hood' has long trumpets centered on large blooms. This sturdy variety is a proven performer in a wide range of conditions.

'Ice Wings' is a Triandrus Daffodil with exquisitely formed, swept-back petals on 12 in. stems. Taller, bolder 'Thalia' has the same shape and adds a clear, sweet scent.

For a different look, try creamy 'Cassata' with a split cup that opens flat. Its lightly ruffled blooms resemble Hibiscus flowers.

The large-cupped Daffodil 'Stainless' is one of the purest whites available, with no yellow tones and just a hint of green at the center.

Naturalized in a woodland

Delicate 'Dainty Miss' blooms

WHERE TO PLANT

White Daffodils are especially versatile in the garden, as they enhance any color scheme. A range of sizes from dainty to bold ensures a selection to suit any setting.

A dark background such as a brick wall or evergreen hedge displays the gleaming petals of White Daffodils best of all. Choose a large variety for the best look in front of a tall hedge.

Against a lush, green sweep of spring lawn, pure White Daffodils stand out and shine brightly. Plant them in large drifts in an area that can remain unmowed until the foliage dies back.

Plant clumps of a fragrant variety of White Daffodils near a path or patio to enjoy their beauty and fragrance when mild spring weather draws you outdoors.

Large, double 'White Lion' with

PERFECT PARTNERS

White Daffodils add freshness to any color scheme and can help to unify multicolored or bright combinations of other spring-flowering bulbs, shrubs, and trees.

Plant the fragrant White Daffodil 'Polar Ice' with citrus-scented, golden orange 'General de Wet' Tulips and pale blue 'Perle Brillante' Hyacinths to perfume the entire garden.

Late-blooming 'Angel' White Daffodils, 'Gravetye Giant' Summer Snowflakes, and Lily-flowered 'White Triumphator' Tulips will bloom together to create a serene, all-white bulb display in late spring.

bicolored 'Merry Widow' Tulips

Under a Magnolia such as 'Dark Shadow', the huge, double blooms of 'Obdam' Daffodils are superb. Rosy Magnolia petals dropping among the white flowers complete a pretty picture.

'Ice Follies' ages to cream

PLANTING & AFTERCARE

YOU WILL NEED: ❏ White Daffodil bulbs ❏ Spade ❏ Compost ❏ Bulb fertilizer ❏ Mulch

1 Plant Daffodils in early fall. Spread a 2 in. layer of compost over planting area; add fertilizer at the rate recommended on the bag.

2 Turn amendments into soil to a depth of 8 in. Mix in thoroughly. Remove and set aside the top 6 in. of soil.

3 Loosen the soil at the bottom of hole, and then level it. Set the Daffodil bulbs in hole 3-4 in. apart, with the pointed ends up.

4 Make sure each bulb is firmly seated in the soil before covering them with reserved soil. Water well. Top with 2 in. of mulch.

5 Deadhead as blooms fade, but wait to remove foliage until it dies back. Topdress with compost and fertilizer each fall.

Tip

Fading is never an issue with White Daffodils. Even gardeners in hot climates can confidently plant them in full sun.

Secrets of Success

BUYING HINTS

● **Buy the largest** available bulbs. Each "nose" on a bulb produces a flowering stem, so double- and triple-nosed bulbs are a good buy.
● **Avoid soft,** bruised, or moldy bulbs. Do not buy any with cuts, which may encourage diseases.

SUN & SOIL

● **Full sun** to partial shade. White Daffodils flower best in full sun, but blooms will last longer in partial shade.
● **Well-drained soil.** Good drainage is essential to keep the bulbs from rotting. Add sand and compost to soil or plant in raised beds.

SPECIAL ADVICE

● **Many White Daffodils** open cream or ivory. They develop their mature, true white in one or two days.
● **Interplant early,** mid-season, and late varieties of White Daffodils in a single clump for a show that lasts through the spring season.

Seasonal Tips

EARLY FALL
Planting & Fertilizing
Plant new bulbs. Topdress established plantings by scratching compost and bulb fertilizer into the soil over the bulbs. In zones 9-11 and warmer parts of zone 8, pre-cool Daffodil bulbs now in refrigerator and wait until winter to plant.

SPRING
Deadheading
Remove faded flowers but leave foliage until it turns yellow to replenish the bulbs for next year's blooms.

EARLY SUMMER
Cleaning up & Dividing
Prune off and compost foliage after it has yellowed. Dig up and divide crowded bulbs *(below)*. Replant immediately, or store in a cool place over summer and replant in fall.

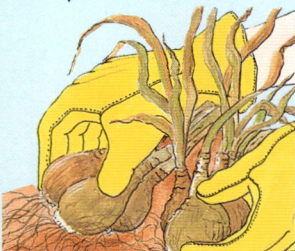

Plant Doctor

Earwigs sometimes infest White Daffodils, eating entire flowers or several large holes. To trap earwigs if they appear in large numbers, place a board on the ground nearby. They will collect under it in the daytime, where they are easy to find and destroy.

Bulbs for Spring Color

*"But who can paint
Like Nature? Can imagination boast,
Amid its gay creation, hues like hers?"*
          —James Thomson

IF YOUR BULBS DON'T COME UP

in the spring, check to see that they're still there—they may have been eaten by squirrels, chipmunks or moles. If you suspect that animals are dining on your bulbs, lay wire mesh on top of the bed. This will prevent hungry critters from digging your bulbs up, but will allow your flowers to grow up through the holes. Another option is to plant Narcissus bulbs around other bulbs—animals don't like the taste of Narcissus and will steer clear of the whole lot.

BONE MEAL IS OFTEN SUGGESTED

as a fertilizer for bulbs, but it's expensive and a complete fertilizer will work just as well. Apply fertilizer after shoots begin to appear in early spring and again after the flowers have died to help fuel next year's growth.

AFTER A FEW YEARS IN THE GARDEN

many bulbs will produce offsets (bulblets or cormels) around their base. These can be divided and replanted to produce more flowers. Divide bulbs after their foliage has died back—usually in late spring.

DON'T WORRY THAT YOUR BULBS

will be harmed by late snow or frost after they've started to bloom. Spring bulbs can withstand freezing temperatures, and even if the flowers do freeze, they will be fine if they thaw out slowly. The only time bulbs may suffer damage from winter weather is if they freeze and thaw out too quickly or if long-stemmed flowers get their stems broken from a heavy snow drift.

ALTHOUGH MANY KITCHEN SCRAPS

will benefit your compost bin, avoid putting meat scraps in the mix. They will most likely attract unwanted animals. Eggshells, coffee grinds, and banana peels are better choices.

The Well-Traveled Tulip

Native to Turkey, Tulips were introduced around Europe by explorers. They were considered great rarities and were sold at exorbitant prices until the Dutch began mass-producing them. The Mennonites brought Tulips to America where they became a symbol of good luck in the hex sign of the Pennsylvania Dutch.

December
- ❏ Force Paper White Narcissi indoors by the first of the month, to enjoy blooms by Christmastime.

January
- ❏ Check mulch around planted bulbs. If strong winter winds are blowing mulch away, keep in place with evergreen branches.

February
- ❏ If desired, bring potted bulbs indoors to force for the spring. Make the transition from outside to inside gradual by putting bulbs in a greenhouse or shed before bringing them into a heated home.

Winter

March
- ❏ Sprinkle fertilizer (5-10-10) over planted bulbs. Leave mulch in place.

April
- ❏ Deadhead early bulbs to improve appearance of garden.

May
- ❏ Remove dead early-bloomers, but leave their foliage until it turns yellow.
- ❏ If dormant bulbs are taking up too much space in your garden, lift and heel them to store later.

Spring

June
- ❏ Remove dead flowers so seed pods don't develop; leave foliage until it's completely dried and yellow.

July
- ❏ Remove dead foliage from early-blooming bulbs that are now dormant.
- ❏ Lift and store tender bulbs that are now dormant.
- ❏ Place catalog orders for bulbs to plant in the fall.

August
- ❏ Many bulbs for fall planting are available now at garden centers. Buy at the end of the month to plant in September.

Summer

September
- ❏ Prepare soil for fall planting, adding fertilizer and organic matter as needed.
- ❏ Plant spring-flowering bulbs.
- ❏ Order bulbs for forcing indoors over the winter.

October
- ❏ Plant remainder of spring-flowering bulbs.
- ❏ Pot hardy bulbs to begin forcing them for winter.

November
- ❏ If weather has not been too cold and the ground is not too hard, you may still be able to plant the last of your spring bulbs.

Fall

INDEX

INDEX

INDEX

INDEX